SURENDORF

Biography of An Artist

Katy M. Tahja

Surendorf Publications

Comptche, California

Surendorf:
Biography of An Artist
Copyright © 2024 by Katy M. Tahja

For information, to order additional copies, or if you wish to purchase original artworks or prints, please contact:

Author Katy Tahja
P.O. Box 194
Comptche, CA 95427
ktahja@mcn.org

Surendorf Publications
Charles Surendorf III
PO Box 216
Comptche CA 95427

Book production by Cypress House
Cover image and page 32: *Self-Portrait*, San Francisco, 2.5×3.5 (1930s) by Charles Surendorf XXX

Publishers Cataloguing-in Publication Data
Names: Tahja, Katy M., author.
Title: Surendorf : biography of an artist / Katy M. Tahja.
Description: First edition. | Comptche, California : Surendorf Publications, [2024]
Identifiers: ISBN: 979-8218308278 | LCCN: 2023920200
Subjects: LCSH: Surendorf, Charles. | Printmakers–United States–Biography. | Painters–United States–Biography. | Authors, American–20th century–Biography. | LCGFT: Biographies. | BISAC: BIOGRAPHY & AUTOBIOGRAPHY / Artists, Architects, Photographers.
Classification: LCC: NE539.S87 T34 2024 | DDC: 769.92–dc23

First Edition

Printed in the USA

2 4 6 8 9 7 5 3 1

First edition

Comments from Art Critics

"Surendorf, an admirable technician in the print block, gives you a perfect sense of the local scene completely felt and beautifully expressed… vigor and shrewd design… extraordinarily detailed and well composed… he sets down the landscape around him with great richness and power and poetic realism."

—Alfred Frankenstein, *San Francisco Chronicle*

"New Orleans scenes are portrayed with a keen sense of dramatic values and sensitive understanding."

—Carter Stevens, *New Orleans Item*

"Every one of his fifty prints in the show has life and an idea. He can cut humor… luminous and living design in black and white."

—Arthur Miller, *The Los Angeles Times*

"Surendorf is something of a satirist—humorous rather than bitter."

—C. J. Bulliet, *Chicago Daily News*

"Repeatedly he makes landscape the subject of keen, compact, and resourceful design."

—Alexander Fried, *San Francisco Examiner*

"The print *Old Captain* is instinct with rhythm and design and rich with the black-and-white contrasts inherent in the nature of the woodblock."

—Albert Reese in the book *American Prize Prints of the 20th Century*

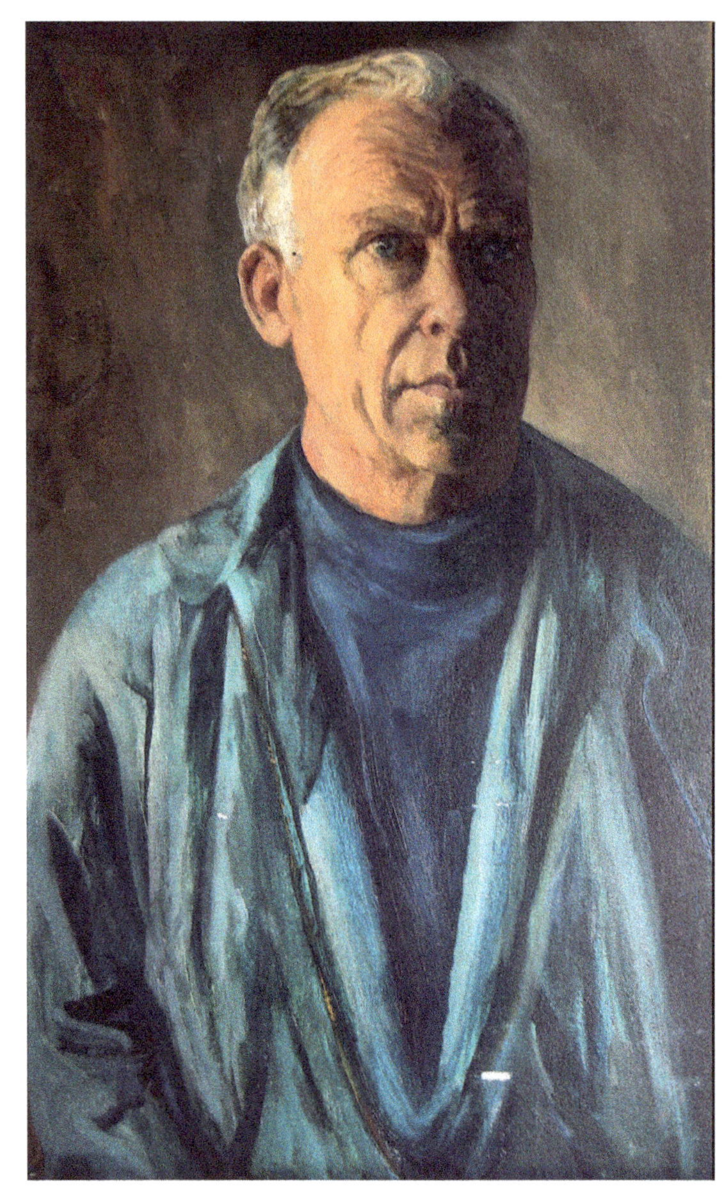

Self Portrait **24×36 (1964).**

Dedication

In appreciation for Mendocino Coast artist James Maxwell who two years ago agreed to meet with me and talk about how to undertake this project. He asked me a very important question: "Who is your ideal reader for this biography?" I replied "There's not just *one* ideal reader for this book, there're many. I want a beginning artist curious to see how one man supported his family all his life with art sales. I want a student of history to see how you can fight the good fight with State Parks and overzealous restoration. I want a reader who likes the story of a free spirit who doesn't like rules. I hope this book finds its way to all those readers.

Also, I dedicate this book to Gallery Bookshop in Mendocino, California. It's a world-class independent bookstore (where I worked for twenty-eight years), and loves to feature books about notable artists.

Illustrations

Table of Contents

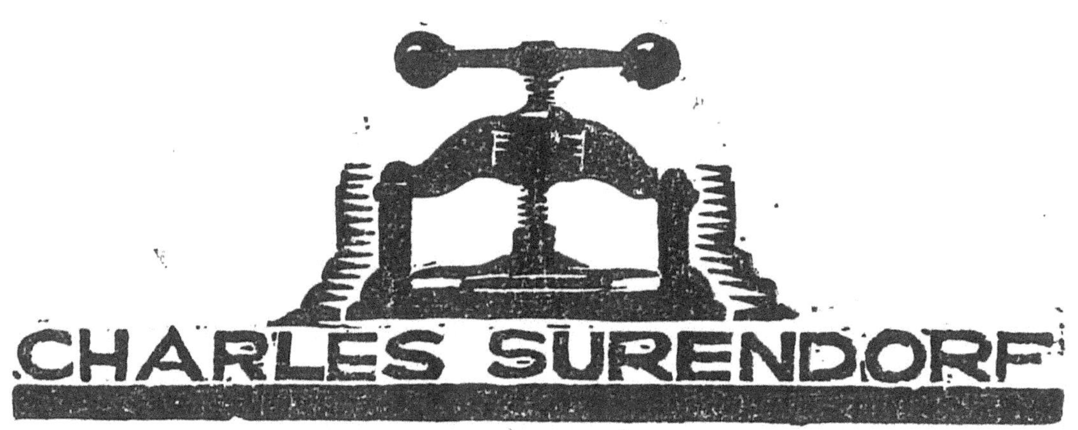

CHARLES SURENDORF

Preface

When writing this volume the author was blessed with access to a 500-page typed autobiography by Charles F. Surendorf II called *Self Portrait in Words.* The artist wrote three separate undated forewords to his autobiography. The following are excerpts from one of those.

I am not a celebrity as are most composers of their own biographies. The art profession I chose early in my life, that of a painter, is not one that is given much notice or acclaim in contemporary times. The autobiographer is not usually pressed for cash but for press clippings. When the limelight starts to grow dim and the stage begins to shrink they panic and grasp a pen.

Surendorf went on:
…there is a sudden realization, after a long visual contemplation in a mirror, that there is such a thing as growing old. I too am possibly guilty of a few of these prompting desires to write. The main reason is that I really enjoy writing every bit as well as painting, and it absorbs my time. The click of this old Remington typewriter is sheer music, and I love the ancient machine because there is not a bit of plastic in its whole anatomy. The fact I have coughed a ton of cigarette ashes into the keyboard does not hinder its mechanical function.

Considering old age in his foreword, Surendorf commented:
It is the companionship of artists that I miss the most. A relationship between artists is as necessary as the stage is to an actor. It is only through constant meetings of sympathetic souls that one in my profession can

function satisfactorily. We give each other's egos the needed bolster that painting can't.

Going on, he suggested:

…a valid reason for wanting to write… the undertaking is a form of therapeutic application. Well aware of my indulgence in an excessive amount of booze in recent years, I knew if I attempted something I considered a serious undertaking, I would have to cool my taste for the grape so that it would not interfere. I know from long experience I can neither paint, nor write, nor undertake any creative work and do it well while drinking. I have tried a thousand times to prove to myself this is not true, and fail every time.

The artist Surendorf also left scrapbooks, poetry, letters, news clippings, and diverse printed materials, including an unpublished novel in the care of his son, Charles F. Surendorf III, in Comptche, California. Hundreds of paintings and prints are housed in a vault in a small home in the redwood forest of Mendocino County. I gleaned this biography from those materials.

A Son's Remembrance

In mid-spring 1979, on one of my last visits to see Dad, I was unaware how severe his lung cancer was. It would bring his death on Memorial Day. In the backyard behind our home were two old barn structures, one a gallery and the other his studio. I learned my fate, being the only Surendorf to carry on the family name, that the contents of the home and outbuildings were to go to me.

For twenty-six years this was rented real estate, but Dad planned for a mobile estate when he passed. He furnished me with the means to build a vault in my house, which was under construction in Comptche, Mendocino County, California. That's where I live today, and that's where Dad's art collection survives.

After fifty years I've decided the collection should be shared with the public. Katy Tahja has been instrumental as a historian and established author in helping me keep a promise I made to my famous artist/father on a sunny day in the foothills near Columbia—that I hoped to write a book about him. He replied, "I hope you do, because if anyone is, you are familiar with my life."

1: Early Childhood

"I have lost much of my memories of the very early days of childhood, submerged out of recollection by the very sameness of the daily routine of meals, school, and play…," says Surendorf in his hand-typed autobiography.

Born in 1906 to an Irish mom, Mary Hurley, and a German dad, Charles Surendorf I, a Pennsylvania railroad locomotive engineer, Surendorf had an idyllic childhood. Raised in the small town of Richmond, Indiana, in the first decade of the last century he lived in the Midwest heartland of America where everyone knew everyone and kids ran free.

When something extraordinary happened he said it was "…boldly engraved upon the mind," like the arrival of Halley's Comet.

> When it appeared in 1910 I was four years old. Its awesome presence in an otherwise placid sky vibrated in my receptive mind each day with conflicting but exciting thoughts. Its coming was like one of my fairy-tale books actually taking place in my own front yard. There were various predictions that it would be nothing more than a fireworks display of splendor, or anticipative anxiety and fear the comet would go off course and hit the Earth.

Charles's nursery school teacher had all the children draw what the comet would look like. The drawing exercise relieved his fantasies. He and his mother walked to the large stone fire engine station where there was a good view of the night sky. Young Charles thought it a fine idea, as there would be all the equipment needed to put out the fire should the comet hit Indiana.

"I can't recall any color in the comet, or maybe I was not color-conscious then. The head of the comet seemed like a billion stars all embedded in a bright ball," he recollected.

Another lasting imprint on Charles's mind was a trip to visit the home of his mom's Irish parents, a hundred miles north near Hartford City, Indiana. Charles's dad, who didn't like to travel, consented to the trip because he had a new Ford touring car. His eccentric driving scared Charles's mom. She remarked often that if Charles senior was in control of any moving object it needed to be on a track.

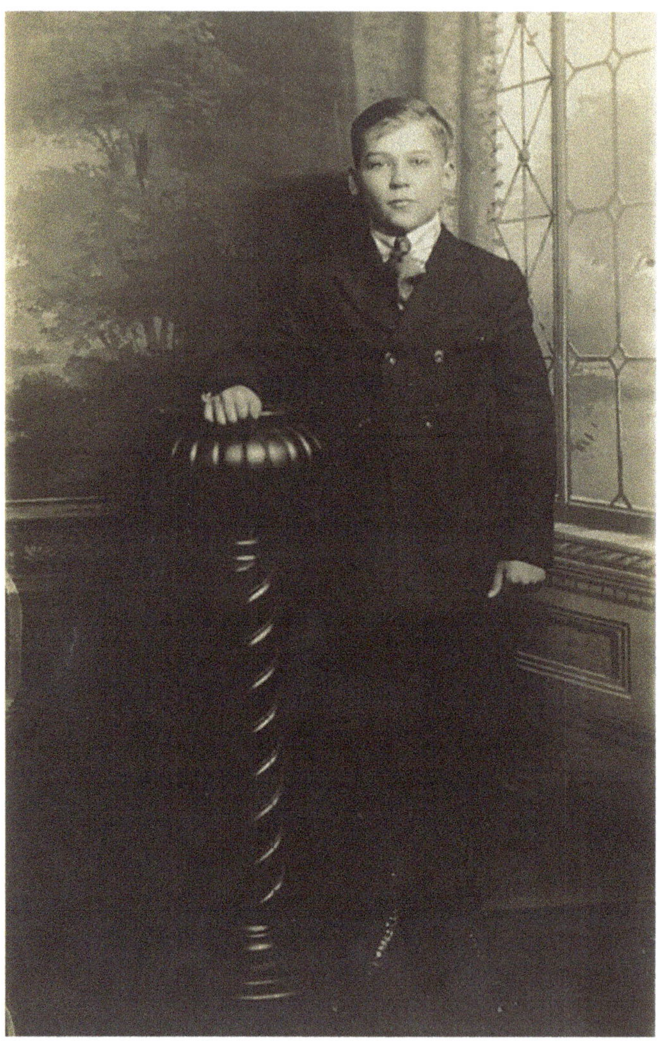

Youth, Charles F. Surendorf, **3×5 (1920s).**

While traveling, Charles Jr. was given his baby brother to hold. When the baby's blanket became damp, big brother cleverly placed the baby in a pocket fold of the car top that was folded down behind the back seat. Mom looked back, saw the baby balanced there, and screamed at Charles Sr. to stop. When Dad turned in his seat to see what was wrong, his driving glove caught the accelerator handle beneath the steering wheel. The Ford jumped forward, and baby Billy bounced up in the air and out onto the gravel road. When he was picked up, the well-padded infant was not crying.

The farm of Tad Hurley, Charles's maternal grandfather, was a poor place with a small unpainted clapboard farmhouse and a tiny barn. "The grandeur of my imagination was blasted to bits," Charles wrote. "She ought to have told me they were very poor. A child has a right to know."

Surendorf liked his grandparents' small home and found a big Holy Bible with snapshots of himself and other family members pasted inside. He went squirrel hunting on a wagon trip to town with Granddad. Charles discovered that the old man collected large cans of garbage to feed the pigs on his farm. Stopping at a small general store, Grandad bought his grandson candy and for himself a quart bottle of "medicine" to soothe his pains.

Charles's mother said drinking was evil; her brother had committed suicide while drunk, and liquor had contributed nothing but unhappiness to her life. Looking back, he believed that Grandma Hurley suspected the devil lurked in hard spirits and made people do things that were not good. "I often wonder if she did not overdo it, making me extremely curious to find out for myself the effect this mysterious fluid possessed," Charles stated. From the wagon ride, young Charles decided two things: drinking was not always evil and could be medicinal, and he never wanted to plant seeds and be as poor as his grandparents.

Thinking back on his dad's work as an engineer, Surendorf recalled, "The element of danger in railroading was the nucleus for the yarns told at the kitchen table. Every story was told with embellished detail of gruesome accidents, wrecks, and horrifying incidents related to unusual experiences."

The young Charles reminisced about his hometown Richmond saying, "My love for the town is pure nostalgia. In growing up there was an uninterrupted pattern of years that made a solid foundation from which to spring. Time tolls slowly in this period to deeply impound even the most trivial emotions into substantial memories."

Fondly remembering his childhood house and as a seven year old he recalled that during World War I, as part of the war efforts his parents rented out a spare bedroom next to his to a young couple. Through a crack in the bedroom door he learned everything there was to know about active sex. "Halley's Comet only comes once every seventy years. It was small potatoes compared to the excitement that went on every night next door," he said.

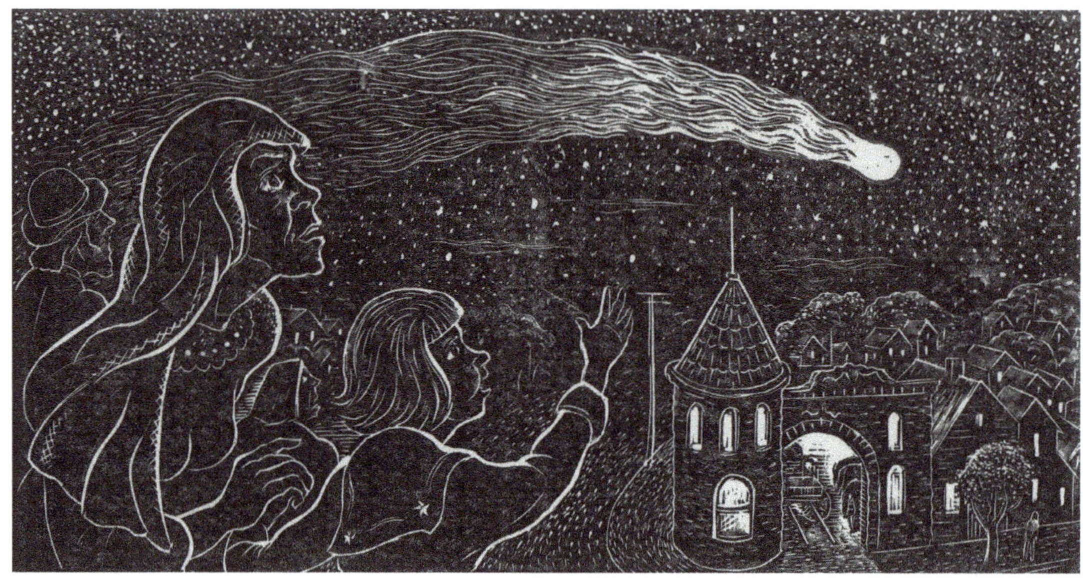

Halley's Comet, **Indiana, 6.25×12 (1940s).**

While in grammar school, for fun Charles produced a weekly two-page newspaper for the neighborhood. The type he used was made of rubber; he made the letters into sentences, then inked the type and stamped it on paper. It took so long to fill two pages that he had little time to do a reporter's job cornering the neighborhood news, so he invented most of it. Once he got in a quarrel with his brother who tore up the papers it had taken him days to print. "I never forgave him," Surendorf said.

There was always part-time work for diligent young men. "I cannot remember a year I did not have some kind of job that provided spending money. Collecting tinfoil during the war for recycling, or owning a shoeshine kit, provided coins." Surendorf also joined newsboys selling newspapers to the soldiers aboard troop trains.

Though it was against railroad company policy, Charles's dad took him for a ride in the cab of the locomotive he operated. His dad always kept his hand on the throttle and the whistle, the firemen never stopped shoveling coal, and the noise was furious, Surendorf recalled. He had a greater respect and admiration for his father after that experience.

2: To Become an Artist

How does one become an artist? Surendorf relates that as a tiny tot listening to someone reading *Little Black Sambo* he felt he had the uncanny power to visualize it so perfectly that it was photogenic. "I was composing all that I heard into concrete and very literal pictures. All I needed was a few sentences, or a paragraph of verbal description, and like magic I could shut my eyes and there would be an actual scene and the event transposed into a fixed image."

One of the best things about his hometown of 25,000 was an established art center that would become the second oldest in the state of Indiana. The Richmond Art Center provided one artist for every 1,000 town residents, and it was not unusual to find framed artwork in every store window on Main Street.

"I had definitely, at the age of ten, decided to be an artist! Just like that! A simple and positive declaration to my parents and friends," Surendorf recalls. He assumed the course ahead would be simple and positive.

"I drew pictures of the park. I drew pictures of everything. I did a self-portrait. I wanted a set of color oil paints and watercolors. I needed brushes and canvases too, but when I learned the prices of art material I bought a bottle of India ink and some pens. I was going to be a cartoonist instead of a landscape painter," Surendorf remembers. He went on:

"Mom let me subscribe to a correspondence course in cartooning. My first lesson arrived and I studied the instructions with more concentration than I exerted in school."

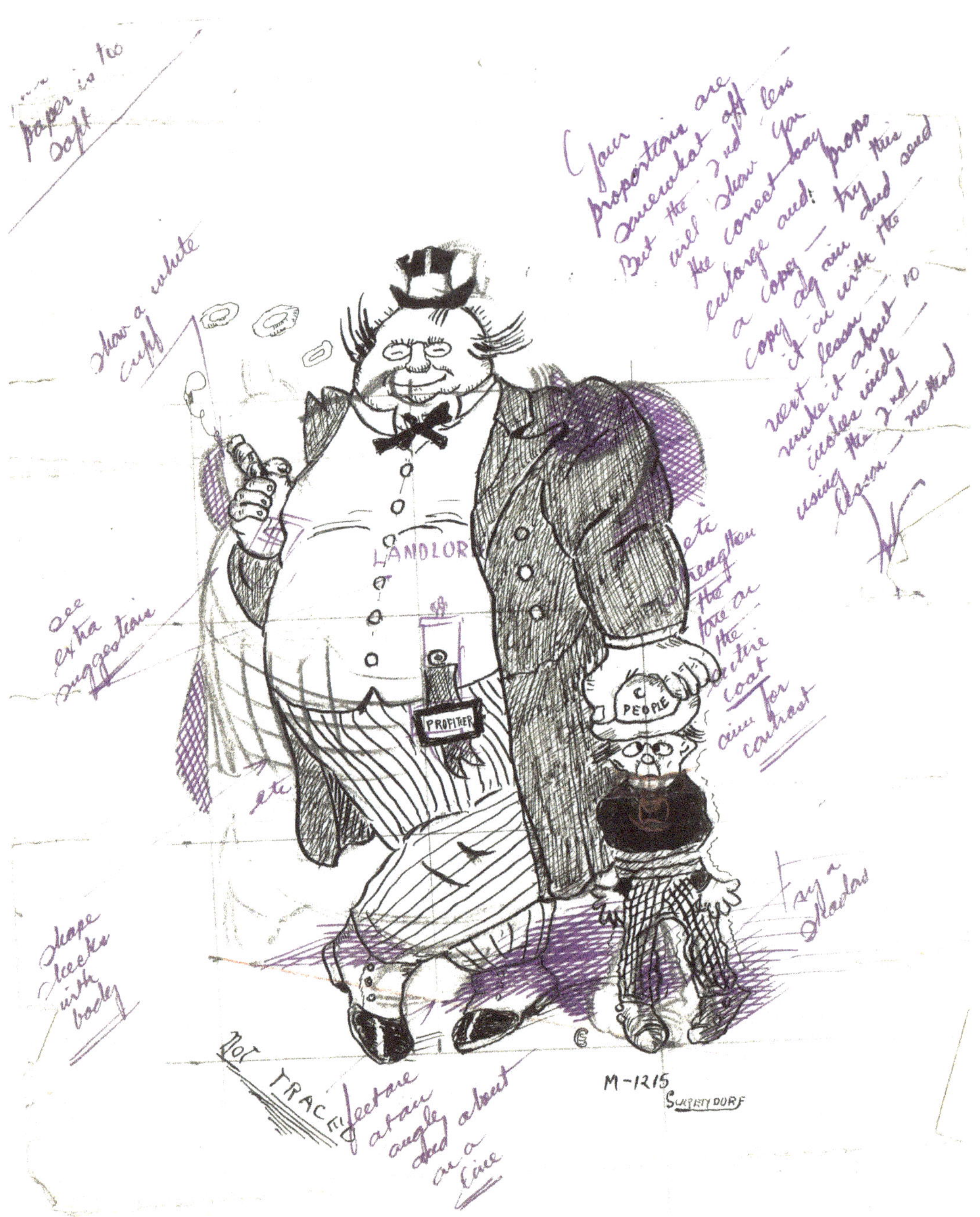

First Cartoon, **Indiana, 8×11 (1920s).**

Then nearly twelve years old, Charles sent his drawings and his first cartoon back to the W. L. Evans School of Cartooning. All were returned with heavy red correction marks and notes. Upset by the criticism, Charles never sent another. He threw those cartoons in the wastebasket and decided to get a good job to pay for paints.

Young Surendorf decided to try for a job at a candy-store soda fountain despite being under twelve. In that era youth needed to be older than that to work late in the evening after school. No luck, so he settled for a job dishwashing, and was able to watch a professional soda jerk and observe the fine art of garnishing. Allowed to advance to preparation of ice-cream sundaes, Surendorf wrote, "It turned out to be sort of an art the way you garnished things with nuts, whipped cream, and maraschino cherries. I caught on fast because I took pride in making each order an extraordinary bit of color and design."

Later he got a job in a drugstore, and bought art supplies with the money he earned. Looking for something big to draw on at home he pulled down roller window shades and decorated them, then rolled them back up. "Dad happened to pull a kitchen blind down and found a funny nude woman milking a cow drawn on it. He didn't think it was funny and I got a spanking," Surendorf wrote.

"Not until I was fourteen and entered high school did the impact of the profession I had chosen have any profound meaning. What made my high school unique was its art gallery. No other high school in the nation had anything like it. The art gallery was larger than most gymnasiums, and high skylights flooded the exhibition hall with soft light," Charles reminisced.

"Another feature of the school was the art classroom. A studio on the north side of the building, where light was even and best to paint in. Few high schools had such working facilities, and the art teachers were experienced and qualified," he said.

Surendorf gave credit to Mrs. Ella Bond Jonston, his teacher: "She has entrée to about every artist studio in the USA, and when she set out to get a painting from an artist she rarely came away emptyhanded."

Well known in art circles, Jonston later administered the art exhibition in San Francisco's Palace of Fine Arts during the Panama-Pacific International Exposition of 1915.

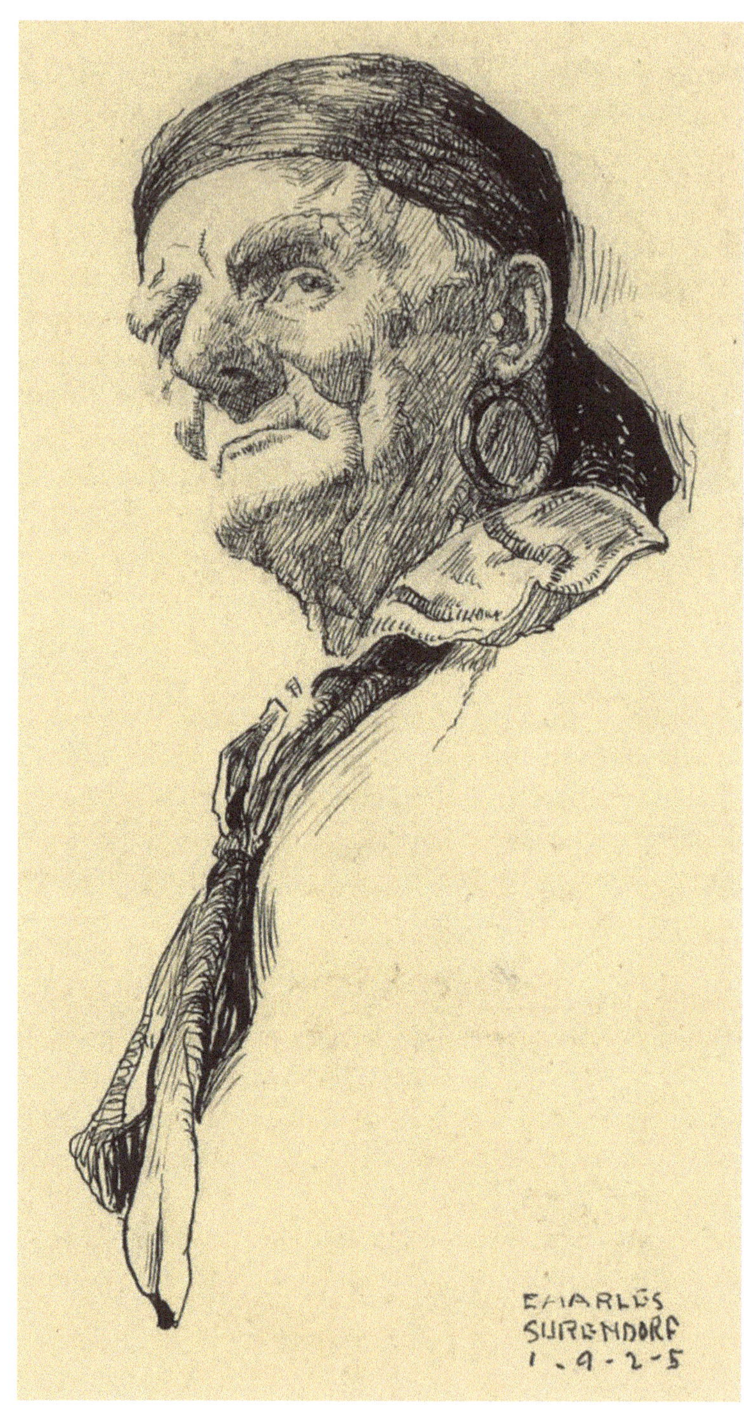

Pirate Sketch, **Indiana, 4×6 (1925).**

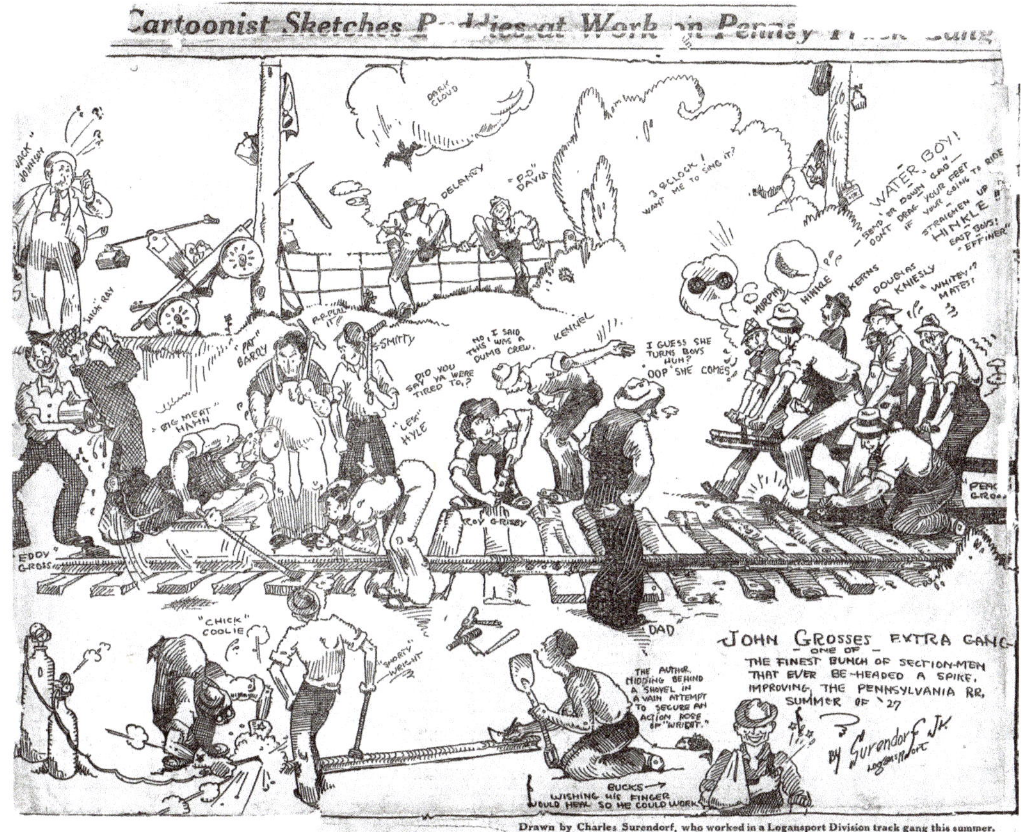

Rail Crew Cartoon, **Indiana, 3.5×9.5 (1927).**

Elaborating, Surendorf says, "Ella realized my interest in art and stimulated the art germ that exploded within me and became a chronic disease. Color and mood seemed to me to be what artists were trying to perfect."

One such artist was John Bundy, dean of the Indiana landscape painters. "An artist who produced accepted market pieces for the public, but loved doing extemporaneous canvases free from preconceived ideas and conventional techniques." Surendorf admitted, "In later years when I returned to Richmond, many things I thought excellent when I was a student now fell flat on their forms. I had overrated them."

A big influence in the teenage Surendorf's life was the acquaintance of Richmond's best-known photographer, Roy Hirshburg. Ten years older than Charles, Roy was half-Jewish, half-Irish, and given to drink. They met because Charles was selling popcorn from a machine in a drugstore and made sketches of customers in his free time. Hirshburg asked to see his work and was impressed. Young Charles was proud that a famous and talented man had seen merit in his art. Some of Hirshburg's work verged into surrealist, and Surendorf remembers, "Being a surrealist in Richmond made you about as popular with arts groups as a man who set up a booze bar outside the tent where Billy Sunday was holding a revival meeting."

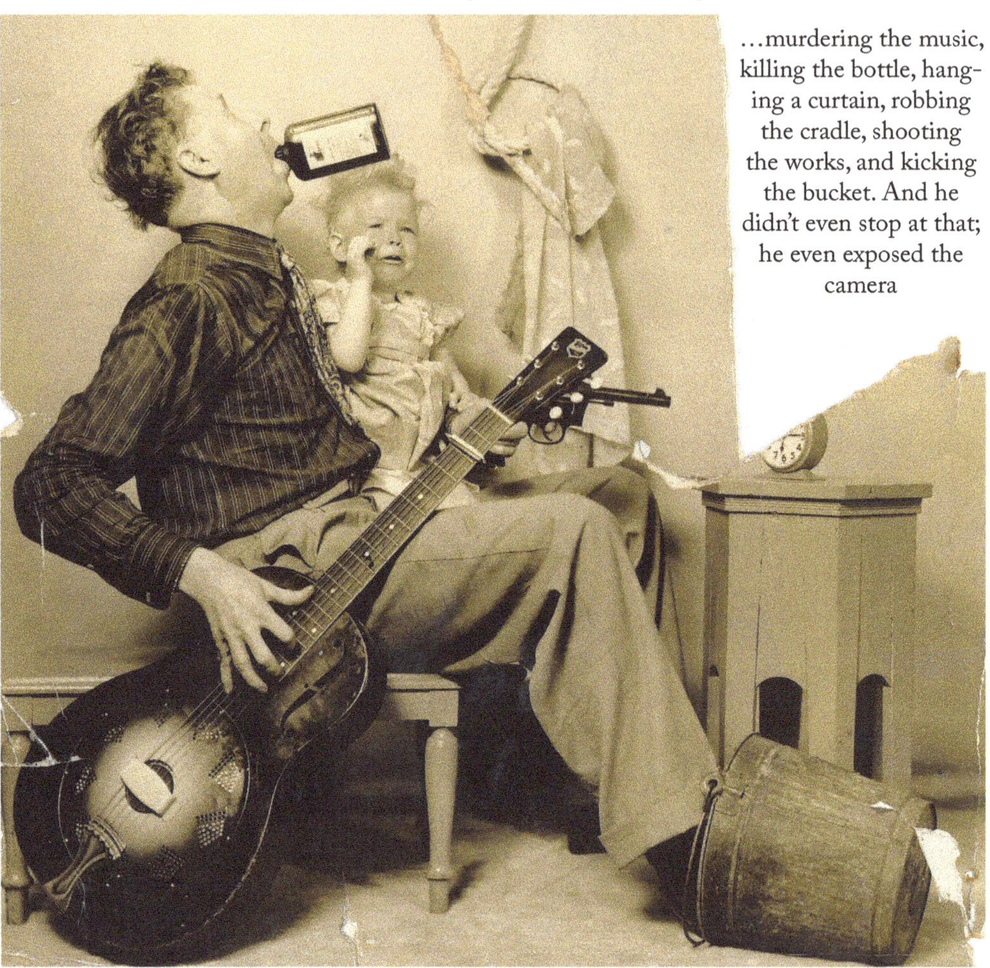

Photo by and of *Roy Hirshburg* (1893–1957). The photo was damaged in a fire.

Surendorf quit selling popcorn and went to work retouching photographs for Hirshburg. He earned one dollar for each negative he retouched and etched, removing the wrinkles and imperfections from portraits. Hirshburg encouraged him to consider art school.

With a free rail pass for a coach seat from Charles's father's workplace, Charles convinced his parents to allow him to go alone to New York City to visit art museums and galleries. He bought a black bowler hat from a haberdashery shop and a pair of gray spats for his shoes to blend in with the crowds and not look like a country bumpkin. "Museum Headache" is the term Surendorf coined for being overwhelmed with images and information on the trip.

Back at work with Hirshburg, Charles was introduced to booze, which would plague him the rest of his life. "I never really felt the influence of booze until I was fifteen. It happened unexpectedly. Without influence, motivation, or precognition. I was busy retouching, alone in the studio, when I found a full pint of minted alcohol. It looked good, it smelled good, and it tasted good too. I got drunk slowly and with great enjoyment," he said. From then on he and Hirshburg were drinking companions. "Our friendship was on a more fluid basis," Surendorf quipped.

Hirshburg had formed a small group of young men into an esoteric club to explore "The Big Idea." Members picked a writer, artist, or musician and had to be able to explain and defend that individual's creativity. For the rest of Surendorf's life he liked to comment on people who possessed a "Big Idea." Hirshburg thought art school should, in the future, be his employee's "Big Idea." He bought the young artist his first set of paints and paid for local art lessons for Charles.

Looking back on the approaching end of his high school years, Charles wrote, "I wasn't particularly fond of school, and the required subjects interested me least of all. The art class was the only one I got a top grade in. I was a bad boy. Not really bad, just too independent and irresponsible."

After the deaths of Charles's two younger brothers, his parents stopped attending church, but even so, Surendorf said, "I am convinced the subtle and carefree youth time is the best and most enjoyable phase of life." Then it was time for art school.

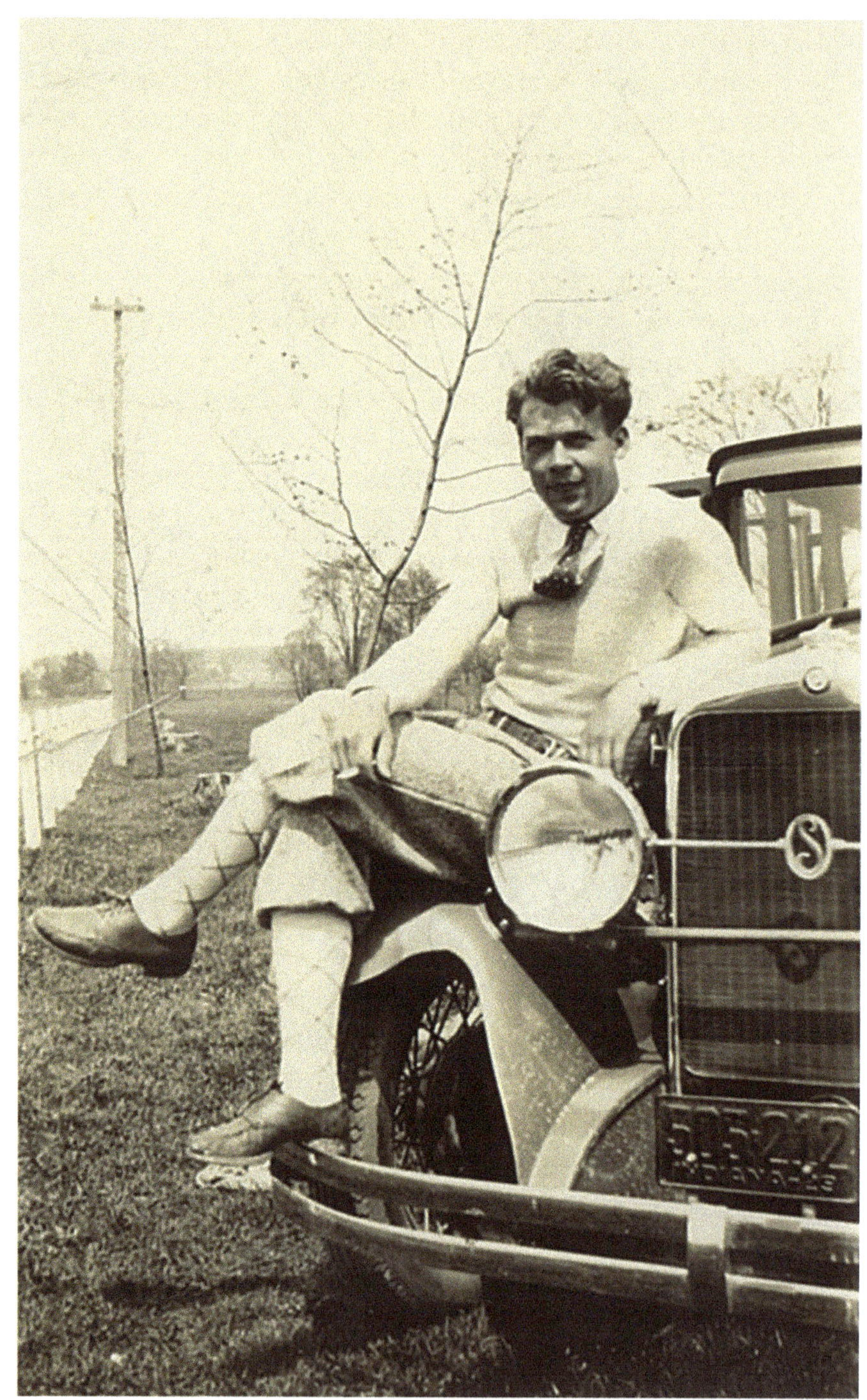

Charles F. Surendorf and Car, **2.5×4.5 (1920s).**

3: Art School

If a student was younger than seventeen, enrollment in the Chicago Art Institute required a notarized parental consent form. Surendorf's mother went with him to Chicago to give consent and see that he got settled in his new home, a room at the South Side YMCA.

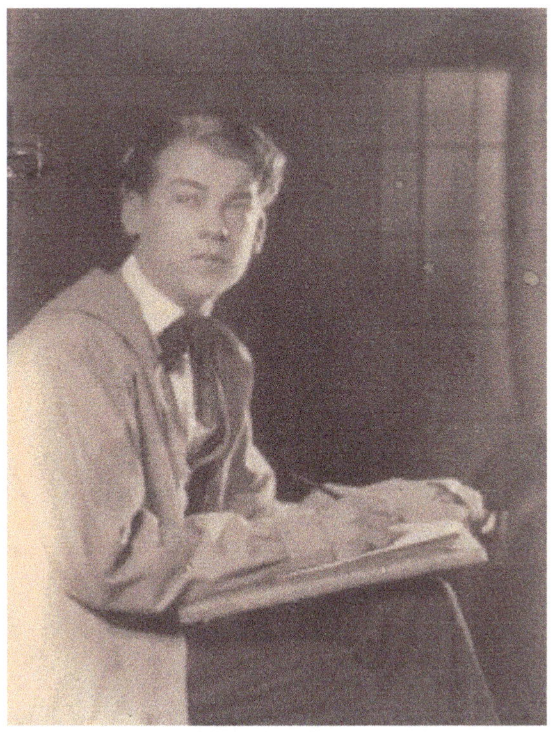

Art School Student, **location unknown, 3.5×2.5 (nd).**

On Charles's first day of school, a nude model fainted; Charles caught her and offered to carry her to the models' dressing room, which involved walking past the main entrance to the museum area from the school quarters. Charles's mother had come to take him to lunch, and as she entered the building, found him with a naked woman in his arms.

Fraternity life in the Roaring Twenties was part of the educational experience; Charles pledged Theta Chi Pi, a group for professional art students. He didn't have the finances to pay room and board in the frat house, but he socialized there. Asked later in life if he'd ever wanted to study in Europe during this time, he said he had little desire to do so as Chicago Art Institute was "the best in the world." After three years of study he was expelled at the start of Christmas vacation—he'd spent too much time doing what he wanted to do and not enough time completing the required courses.

Attending classes with the Art Student League in New York City was his next goal. With his parents covering his rent, he got a job and free meals at a B/G sandwich shop and looked forward to a summer job as a section hand doing construction work—paying forty cents an hour—on the railroad where his father was employed. In 1926 Charles had returned to the Midwest to attend Ohio State University. By the end of the school term he was broke, unable to live within his means, and said, "I did what I swore I would never do, and went to work in an advertising agency. The lettering I learned in the institute came in good stead. I wasn't prostituting my talents; I was applying my education." He drew cartoons for the campus humor magazine, and with that income he rented a room in one of the better homes near the school.

"The Roaring Twenties had just about roared itself out," Surendorf said. Again, he got restless, quit work and school, and shipped his bags home. In 1928, after three attempts at higher education, Surendorf and a friend planned what every Midwesterner wanted to do once in their lives—visit California.

4: Cross-Country Hitchhiking

Hitchhiking was a new and unexplored form of travel that they wanted to try. "The rule of the highway was to travel light and dress like you were going to church. I wore tweed, plus-four knickers [i.e., shorts that extend four inches below the knee], and scotch-plaid stockings," Surendorf said.

The first day, they traveled 300 miles to St. Louis. Charles spotted a B/G sandwich shop. He told the manager they were on their way to California and that he had worked his way through art school in a B/G. They got free food.

Charles's traveling companion had an Irish surname, and in a stroke of genius the pair had obtained a letter of reference from the Irish mayor of their hometown attesting to the fact they were young men from reputable families and were off on an adventure. More than once they showed that letter to cops who'd found them sleeping in a city park. Sometimes, small-town sheriffs even gave them rides in police cars.

"Hitchhiking is an extremely tiresome and trying form of transportation," Surendorf admitted. "One time we got a ride in what must have been the worst mobile heap on Highway 40," a broken-down old Hudson with two men in the front. The men questioned them on how much money they had. "We answered, 'We wouldn't be hitchhiking if we had any money,'" and got dropped off as soon as possible. They slept in a deserted baseball grandstand and a jail once, and visited YMCAs to shower.

In Denver, Surendorf called a fraternity brother from the Chicago Art Institute; he gave them a clean soft bed for one night. In Phoenix, after a long, disappointing wait, they took a ride in a Model T Ford with two cushions strapped to the gas tank in front for seats, and a soapbox tied over the rear axle for a back seat. They were tired, hungry, and thirsty, and blasted by dust, sand and sunshine, but they were on their way to Los Angeles!

Eight days after they'd left one Main Street in Indiana, they chugged to a halt on another Main Street in L.A. and headed for a YMCA. Their parents sent them clothes and Surendorf's portfolio of art-school drawings. His travel companion found a job, and Surendorf went to cousins in Pasadena for a few days. He was not enchanted with California, however, and headed back to Indiana as quickly as possible. "I really felt elated to be going home. It seemed to be a waste of time to hang around California. Nothing appealed to my artistic eye. I did get a good feeling out in the desert… that stirred my painter's instincts."

Hirshburg and his friends were surprised to see Charles back so soon. "To these Hoosiers, California was utopia," Surendorf mused. He described people in Los Angeles as identical transplants of hundreds of ordinary Midwesterners. The only noticeable difference was palm trees. After the hitchhiking trip he decided:

> I wanted to imbed myself within the very heart of nature. It had not taken long to realize that my creative urge was best fulfilled when the purest poetic forms of nature were revealed. Nature becomes more poetic when divorced from manmade backdrops. It's beautiful, mysterious charms seem to generate and radiate the essence of the intangible something artists seek. When one is alone with nature, one becomes more of a part of it.

After his hitchhiking adventure, Charles wanted to live alone. For this new escapade he found a deserted, decrepit farmhouse on the banks of a river near his parents, and in a routine he would practice for the rest of his life, traded his artwork—in this case, two oil paintings for a year's rent. His parents let him charge his groceries on their account at a nearby store. He had no refrigeration, and hunted and fished for his dinner. Milk was ten cents a quart from the farmer next door, where the farmwife baked him bread for ten cents a loaf. On rainy days Charles wrote poetry; otherwise he painted.

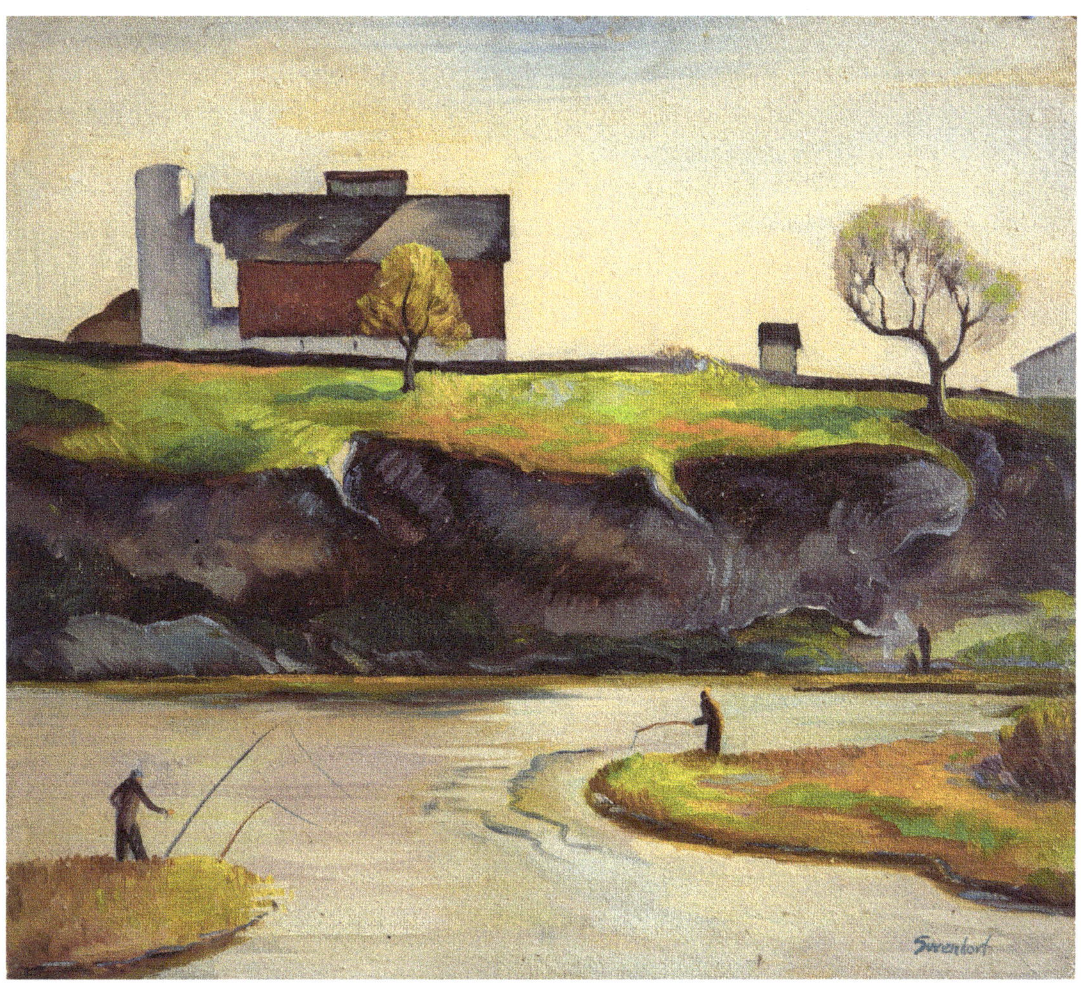

Wabash River, Indiana, 22×20 (1930s).

A friend gifted him a box of German pastels. "I had never seen such a division of tones," he recounted. "Every color in the spectrum was there from the most brilliant down to the softest tones imaginable. I must have done over a hundred drawings before the chalky colors were exhausted." He wrote a mail-order art-supply company in Indianapolis and found the pastels hadn't been manufactured for fifty years and had been very expensive when they'd been on the market.

Surendorf enjoyed the undemanding freedom of being alone and looked forward to uninterrupted hours to work. He had been determined to spend the winter in the old house, but, out of food and cigarettes, he said "To hell with it. I had exhausted the subjects to paint near the house. I longed for companionship of other artists and authors. I wanted a drink of booze." He moved back to his parents' home in Logansport. "All I cared about was catching up on all the stupid earthly pleasures I had denied myself to live alone."

Surendorf's parents would pay for his comfort and food, but not his booze. When he threw a party in his parents' home when they were out of town, they found out and kicked him out. In his old town of Richmond, he acquired a job making stencils and drawings for a local magazine. With his first paycheck he rented a two-room studio for $10 a month. With four large windows it was an excellent place to paint. He started to offer weekend art classes at $1 a lesson.

While working as a cartoonist for a local publication in the Midwest in 1928 and 1929, he visited his old fraternity house in Chicago, where an admirer, seeing some of his portfolio, invited him to come to Los Angeles to collaborate on a new series. The offer was from Walt Disney, and the series was the first Mickey Mouse cartoon. First, however, Charles had to raise the $35 train fare—and he couldn't do it.

5: An Opportunity Lost, Another Gained

Surendorf missed his chance to get in on the ground floor of the Disney empire, but forty years later he visited Southern California and thought that the studio looked like a churning factory of people drawing small sections of a story. "It was not art. I couldn't have stood it," he said.

Picking up yet again, he moved south to Crawfordsville to study with painter Fritz Schlemmer. After examining a sample of Surendorf's previous work, Schlemmer said, "There is nothing wrong with the color and composition, but someday you will realize you have gone no further. This painting will be just as good as the one you paint years from now if you stay in this groove, but it has nothing of aesthetic value. Its content is cosmetic and shallow. Surendorf, it will take a lot of living and a lot of painting to get your Big Idea."

The young artist looked at his painting on the easel. "It was really sweet," he recalled. "The buildings were actually old and ugly with age. Beauty, another evasive element, was there. I saw it, but I hadn't felt it. I hadn't told the truth about the real thing because I did not have the eye or mind to express the essential. I had converted a powerful subject into a pleasant calendar picture. "I'll need a lot of time," I said. "I was fortunate to have as my first professional painting guide a man such as Fritz…. He instilled a reverence and respect for art at a down-to-earth level. I am indebted to him… he was more than a teacher; he was a prophet."

In 1932 Franklin D. Roosevelt was elected president, and in 1933 Surendorf decided to try his luck in Washington, D.C. He hoped to join artist acquaintances in a shared studio space, but that didn't work out; instead, he found a room on

DuPont Circle for $20 a month. His mom lent him $5 a week, and he hoped to pay the rest by painting pictures. He organized an outdoor art show, but had no luck, as he priced his paintings too high and nothing sold.

Want to get free food in a big city? Attend the opening of an art exhibition in a gallery. These receptions provided Charles free meals as he crashed parties and ate hors d'oeuvres while mingling with congressmen, diplomats, and dignitaries. He also impersonated a restaurant provisions buyer. While walking the nearby river wharves where fishermen had wholesale outlets, he sampled oysters to his heart's content.

At the Corcoran Gallery of Art, Surendorf submitted one of his Indiana paintings to the Biennial Exhibition. It was accepted! "I was hanging alongside some of the best artists in the United States. I was still a punk kid, but it was a damn good painting."

Again, nothing was inspiring his painting instincts, but fellow artists found escape in the Youghiogheny Forest Colony in West Virginia, where there was a cabin resort that had closed during the Great Depression. The resort owner hoped having artists living there would make it more alluring to tourists. Charles packed up in Washington, filled the trunk of a friend's car, and they took off for the hills. He suddenly felt like painting again. "With Prohibition over, the price of moonshine came down," he recalls. "I still preferred moonshine to legal booze. I would always strain the bugs and flies out of the illegitimate stuff before I poured a drink. This crap about mountaineers drinking the booze out of tin cups and jugs like it was water has got to be baloney. A tin cupful would have had me uprooting trees."

President Roosevelt established programs to provide financial relief through work, and he gave consideration to artists. Charles, visiting his parents in Indiana, found that a $500 relief check had been delivered for him. It was to be an advance on an oil painting to be given to the government. Surendorf had totally forgotten he had ever applied to the U.S. Treasury Department to be part of the project. Art supplies and a brand-new double-breasted suit from the best men's clothier in town used up the money. When it was time to turn the painting in to the John Herron Art Institute in Indianapolis, Charles dug out a snow scene he'd painted years ago. This painting for the Treasury Relief Art Project was installed over the fireplace in the Richmond Library. Unfortunately, the library later burned down.

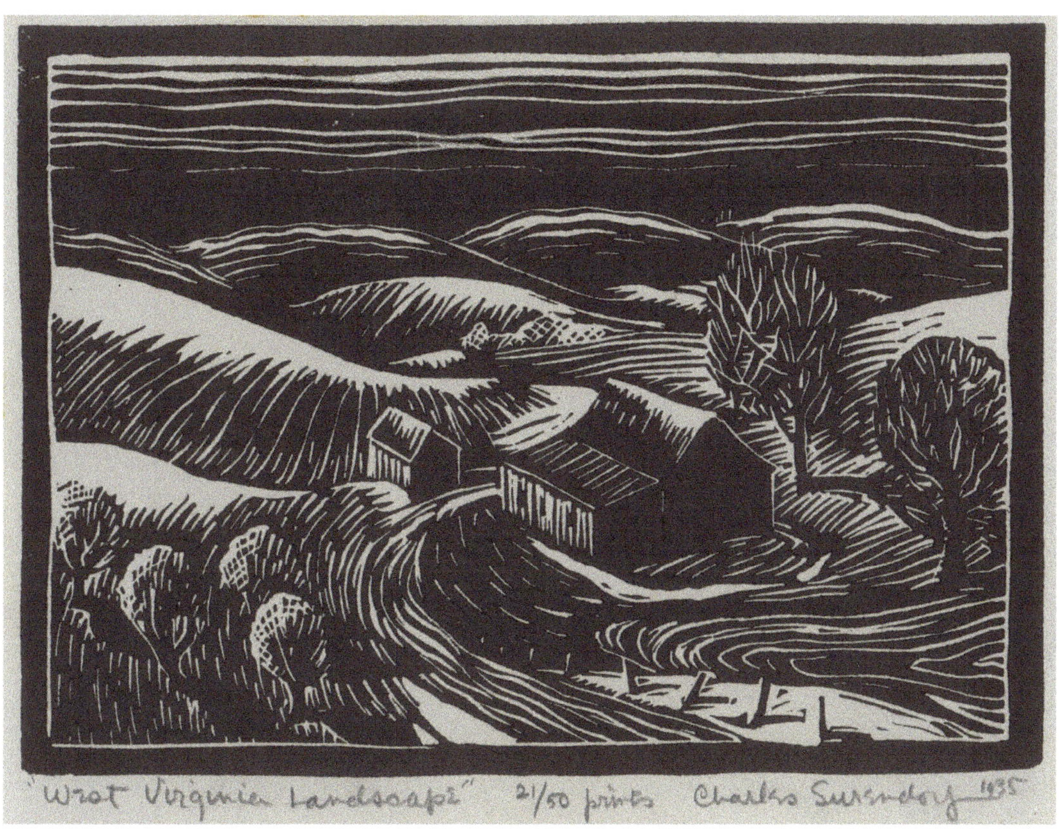

West Virginia Landscape, **5.5×7 (1930s).**

Chapter 6: The Printmaker

Artist Charles Barnes was ten years younger than Surendorf, and worked as an attendant at the Richmond High School Art Gallery where Charles had paintings on display. Barnes, Surendorf, and Hirshburg liked to meet and talk art. Again, Surendorf exchanged art lessons for rent on a small cottage. At this time he tried making his first block print. "I didn't know a damn thing about printmaking, but it fascinated the hell out of me." One thing he found hard to learn was cutting the alphabet letters in reverse on the blocks. "It was one of the most enjoyable periods of my life. I was so interested in the effects of various techniques and the unlimited possibilities of black and white that color held no interest."

Hand printing presses were used in lawyers' and railroad express offices to duplicate documents. The presses became obsolete with the invention of carbon paper. In 1935, Charles bought a used press, experimented with printing, matted some prints, and sold his first works for less than $1. "Museums and galleries were desperate for exhibitions of contemporary art," Surendorf noted. "You could get a showing anywhere in the country, but you couldn't count on sales. Nevertheless, I made a good living peddling my prints. During the Depression I traded paintings and prints for about anything I needed, and I taught art classes with funds allocated from an appointed county committee for the arts."

His students were young housewives and unmarried teachers. He got fined for dating students and for showing up for class drunk one night. While staying briefly at a cabin at Lake Maxinkuckee near Culver, Indiana, Charles observed turtles crawling on white sand at the water's edge. Their shells were the size of human faces. Surendorf dove down, caught the turtles, dried them off, then painted human faces that covered the shell. When they were dry he placed the turtles back in the lake. "It sure looked wild to see faces moving around under the water," he joked.

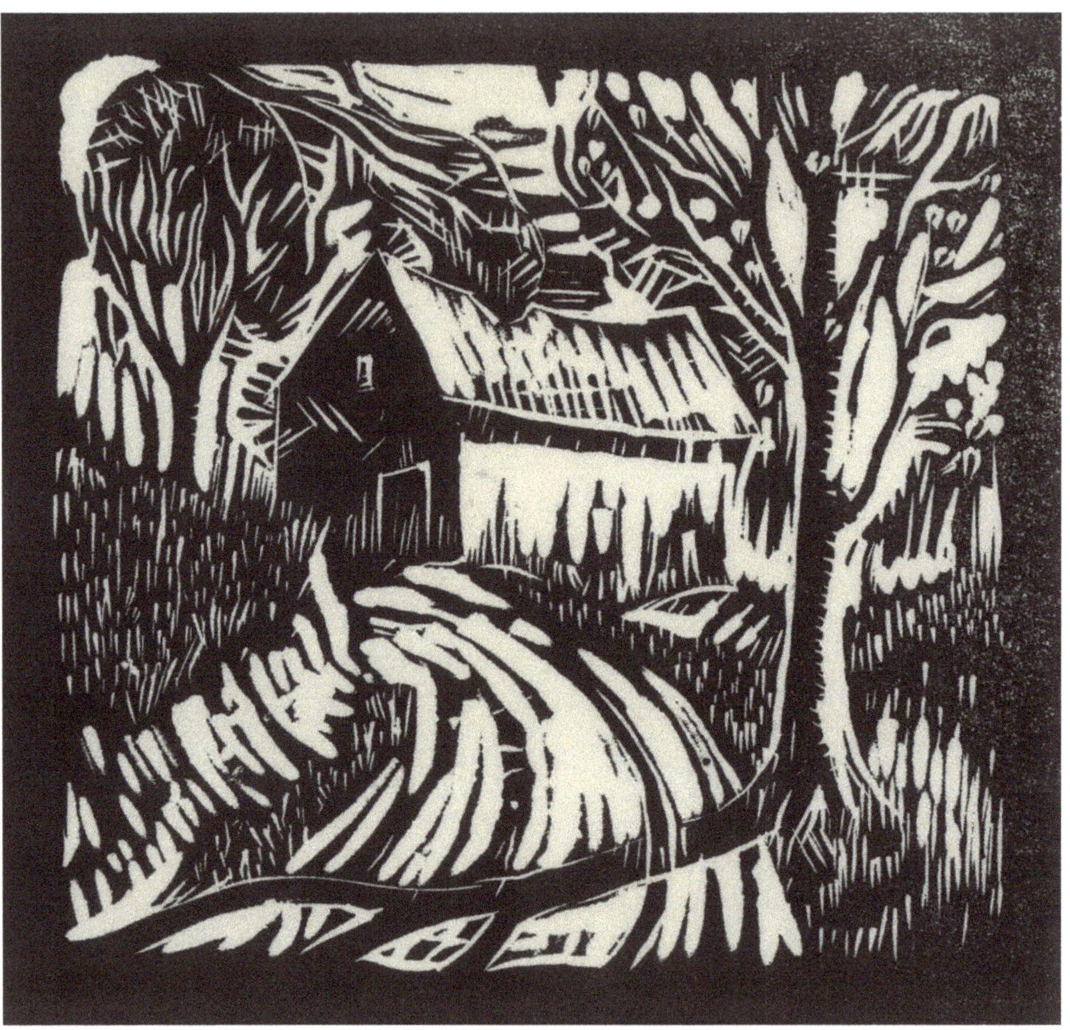

First Block, **4.75×5 (1934).**

At this time he met Charles Safford, an artist who would become a lifelong friend. Safford invited Charles to the Coachella Valley desert in California. To make expenses, Surendorf matted prints and sent them ahead to the Paul Elder Gallery on Post Street in San Francisco. He went on to exhibit there for years. Surendorf tried to get a free railroad pass because he still lived at home with his locomotive-engineer dad, but by then was too famous and had garnered too much publicity, so he spent $30 on a coach train ticket to Indio, California.

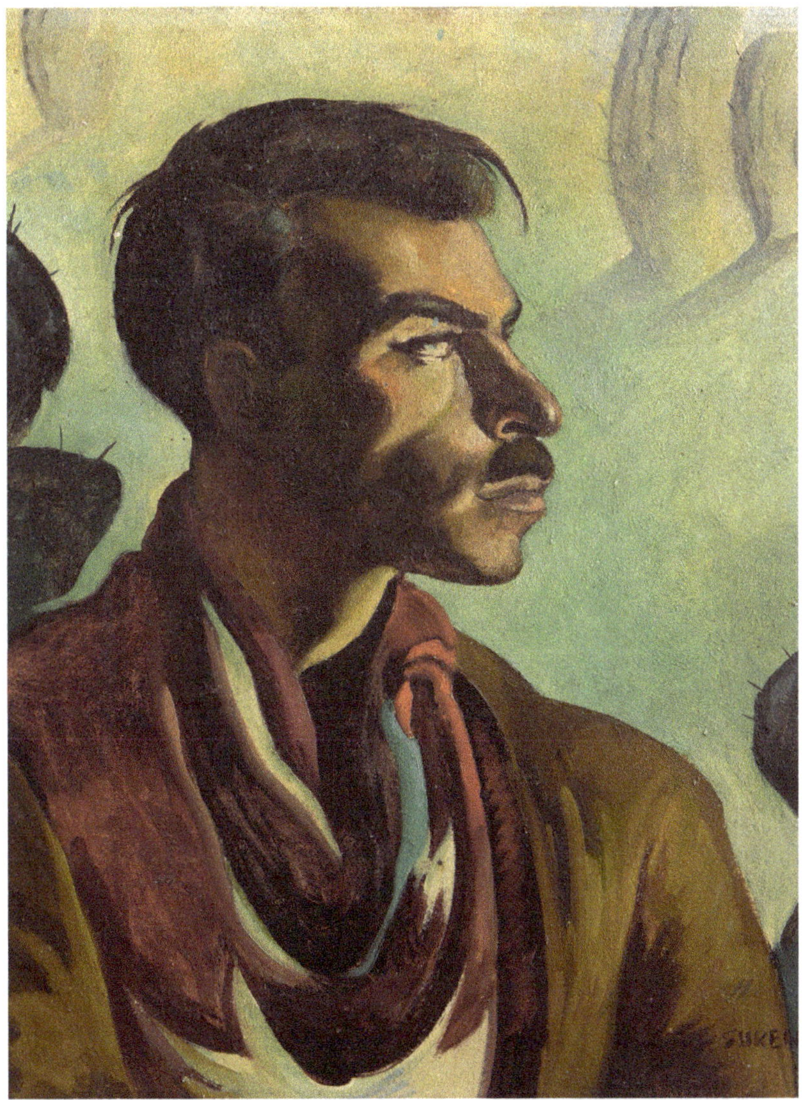

Charles Safford, artist and friend, **24×36 (1930s).**

Safford lived in an adobe house, a former trading post, and paid his rent in paintings. The artist had so many friends passing through that he'd made one room a dormitory. It seemed every car on the highway on its way to Palm Strings stopped to visit. Surendorf said, "The desert has a mystic essence. I found myself engulfed in an unsought love affair. I painted better and lived happily." When the summertime weather got too hot for painting, Surendorf wrote home for train fare. His dad's response was "Try hitchhiking."

He boxed his paintings and prints and planned to send them by railway express, but the fee was $35 and he had only $30 in his pocket. He unpacked the paintings, took the oils out of their frames, sandwiched them between cardboard, tied rope handles on the cardboard, and declared it a suitcase. A coach ticket cost $30 for him and his "suitcase." Once the train was underway, he dressed in his best suit, unpacked some prints, and went into the first-class club car where he sold them for $1 each and made spending money.

7: Pacific Travels and New Romance

After a visit home with his parents in Indiana, Charles bought a ticket for the *City of San Francisco* train. "I decided to go someplace I had never been before." He didn't know what San Francisco would be like. The train stopped in Oakland and he boarded the ferry to cross the bay. "I was spellbound by what I was seeing," Surendorf recollected. "I had no idea there was a city in my own country so lovely to view from such an unusual vantage point as the rolling ferry boat."

There were no smoke clouds in the sky like Chicago and Indianapolis. He saw a cloudless clear sky and felt a soft, warm wind. The hills in the city were almost obliterated by thousands of white buildings. "San Francisco did not wait for me to land on its shore. It reached out and seized me. I welcomed its embrace with deep affection."

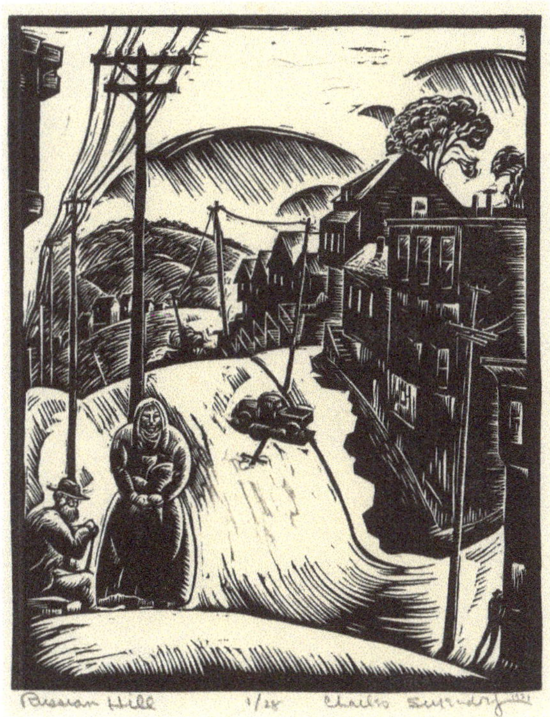

Russian Hill, San Francisco, 6.25×7.5 (1930s).

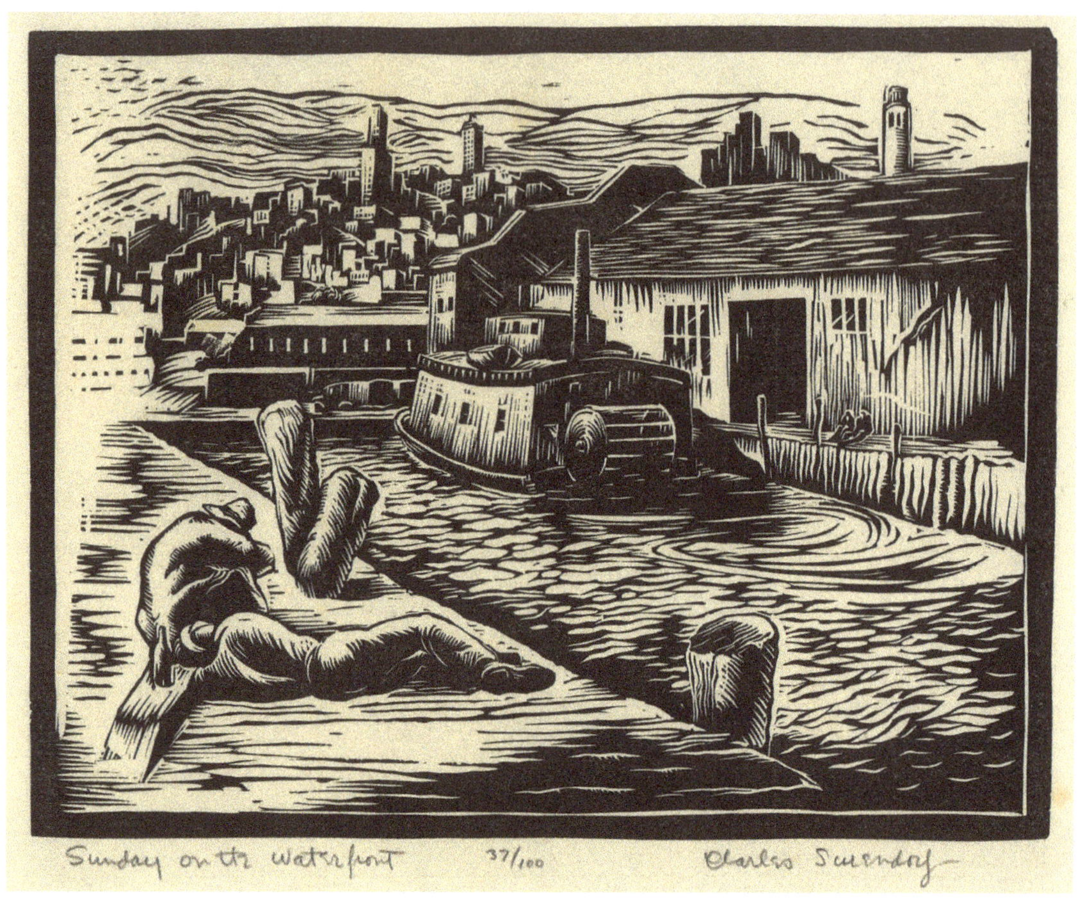

Sunday on the Waterfront, **San Francisco, 8×10 (1930s).**

Having found a cheap room to rent, he didn't start job hunting for the first few days; he was just happy to walk around looking at the town. "A thousand subjects loomed as paintable," he observed, but didn't unpack his paints. He resolved never again to write home for help from his parents.

Surendorf walked the San Francisco streets looking for Help Wanted signs. Checking in with the Paul Elder Gallery, he found that none of his prints had sold. On Sunday, August 11, 1936 he put a classified ad in the Positions Wanted By Men column of the *San Francisco Examiner:* "Artist Surendorf wants any kind of position" with a box number at the newspaper. He actually received a reply from a former classmate from the Chicago Art Institute who offered him a free studio.

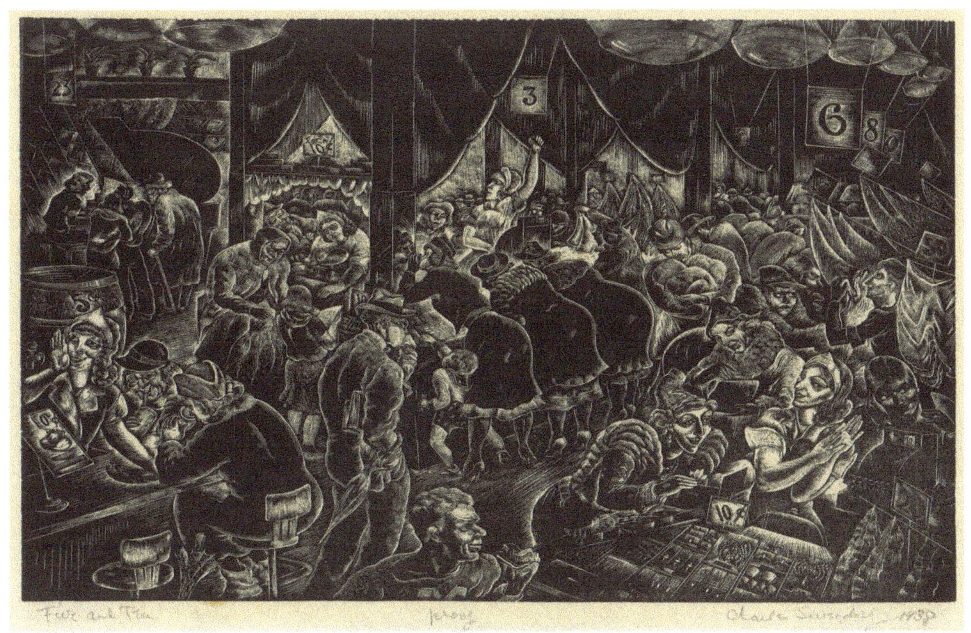

Five and Dime, **8.5×11.75 (1938).**

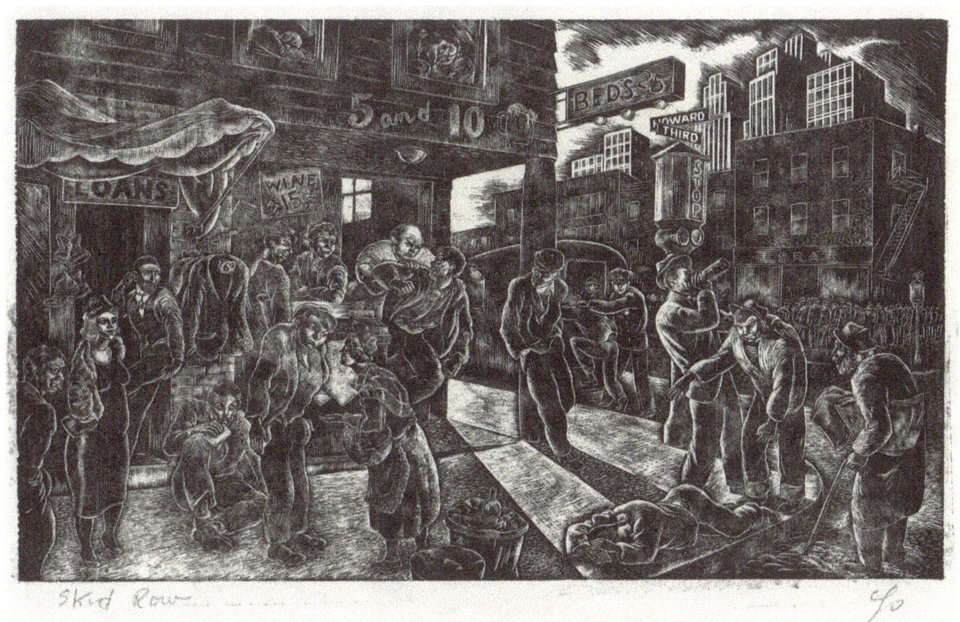

Skid Row, **San Francisco, 8×12 (1937).**

Paddlewheel river steamers traveled from the Bay Area to Sacramento. Surendorf drew the boat tied up at the wharf with an unemployed sailor asleep on the deck. He turned the sketch into a block print, and sent it to an exhibition in New York City called "America Today." A book of 120 prints from the show was published, including his. "I became a 'native' San Francisco artist in less than six months," he said.

The San Francisco Museum of Art was the last place Surendorf would ever have expected to find a job, but that was where he ended up. He became a museum attendant, a tasteful way of saying "guard." He walked long corridors through various galleries to be sure none of the masterpieces were stolen. "It was a hard and empty job—ten hours a day on your feet on cold marble floors," he recalled. "There is no work more stifling than guard duty in a museum. Whoever set the pattern for the design of museums must have been a descendant of the macabre individuals who invented torture racks."

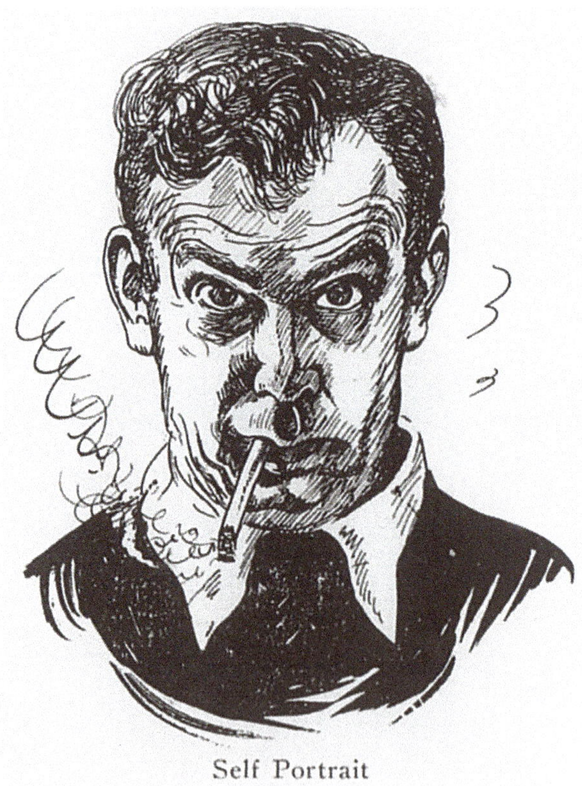

Self-Portrait, **San Francisco, 2.5×3.5 (1930s).**

"The only thing that bugged me about San Francisco was the color quality of the landscape and buildings. It lacked a certain richness and warmth of color one finds in other parts of the nation's country and urban areas," Surendorf mused. "It just wasn't paintable, although the compositions nature and man presented together were terrific. I have never seen a painting of San Francisco that wrapped it up. It might have been the prevailing veneer of fog and haze that obliterates the substance of color quality."

Surendorf joined Paul Elder and his wife to walk across the Golden Gate Bridge on its opening day. On days off he took the ferry to Sausalito to paint watercolors. A fellow artist, a curator at Gump's department store art gallery, told him about a great place to sketch, an old ghost town from the goldmining era in the Sierra foothills called Columbia.

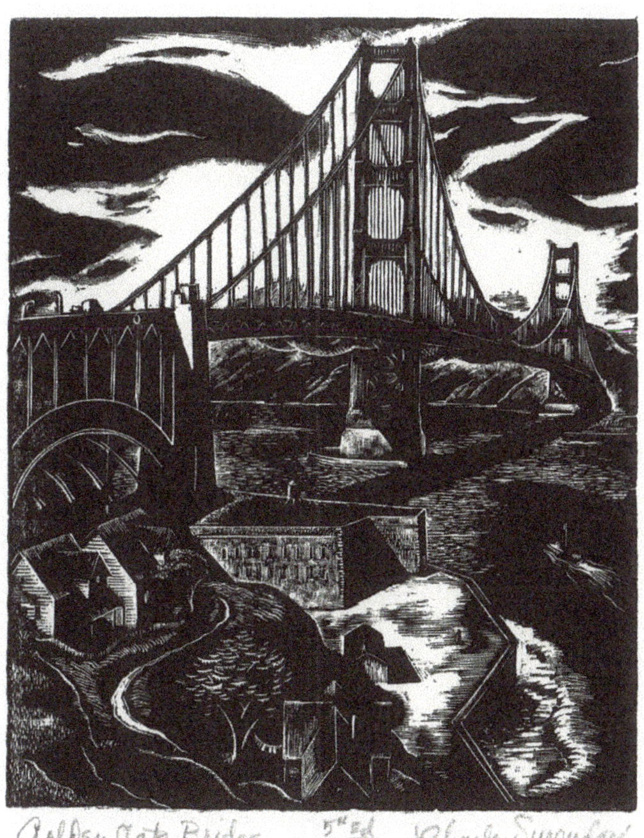

Golden Gate Bridge, **San Francisco, 4.75×6 (1930s).**

A first visit to Mother Lode country had him considering it "weird in a beautiful way… not a car or a person was in sight on the streets of Columbia… it looked like a deserted movie set." Surendorf found it was a painter's paradise as he explored the main street and the back roads that circled the town. Brick buildings had caved-in roofs and massive iron doors. The town came alive at four in the afternoon when the mail was delivered to the post office. He found the old town the best preserved of all the gold camps and a monument to the past. The quality of paintable subjects was unlimited. He planned to come back. The museum promoted him to the installation department, but the job bored him. He learned about running a gallery and managed to accumulate a nest egg of money, but then quit to go back to Indiana for the holidays.

The Federal Arts Program was a Depression-era government program that employed artists to make art for public buildings and spaces. Surendorf had to be a certified welfare case, flat broke and hungry, which proved easy. His first assignment was to do detailed drawings of wildflowers for six weeks before he was reassigned as a printmaker.

"The end-grain woodblocks were the finest. It was wood from the Arabian Box shrub, the hardest wood in the world. The tools were of German steel, and they gave us an unlimited supply of paper and ink. It was Christmas," Surendorf enthused.

For every 2,500 prints he made from his blocks he was allowed to keep three. He had to attend a monthly meeting where he turned in completed prints, was given new materials, and collected a $100 check. Artists had unlimited freedom to work as they pleased. Surendorf bought an old hand-operated letter press for $5 that was the largest size ever made. He kept it the rest of his life and joked that he wouldn't sell it for $10,000.

An art student named Joan Brambila (1918–2015) shared Charles's life for a year, but he took to drinking too much, which irritated the heck out of the young woman. Together they took trips from Carmel to the Trinity Alps in California. Surendorf took classes at Mills College in figure and portrait painting.

"I still thought of doing prints as a sort of rainy-day hobby. My first love, my professional ideal, was painting. Most printmakers are painters too. You strive for the same principles in prints that you do in painting. Good compositions, tonal harmony, contrast of light and dark and mood and feeling," Surendorf said.

During the winter of 1937–1938 he carved numerous linoleum blocks because he wanted to be able to keep them. Woodblock engravings were submitted to the

Federal Arts Project. By spring, Surendorf had a new idea. Inspired by neighbors he contemplated a round-trip to Tahiti.

"I found it hard to believe they could become so passionately fond of a distant dot on the landscape." Of his neighbor he said, "When they spoke of the calm lagoons that reflected exotic mountain peaks, I itched to paint it." Planning started.

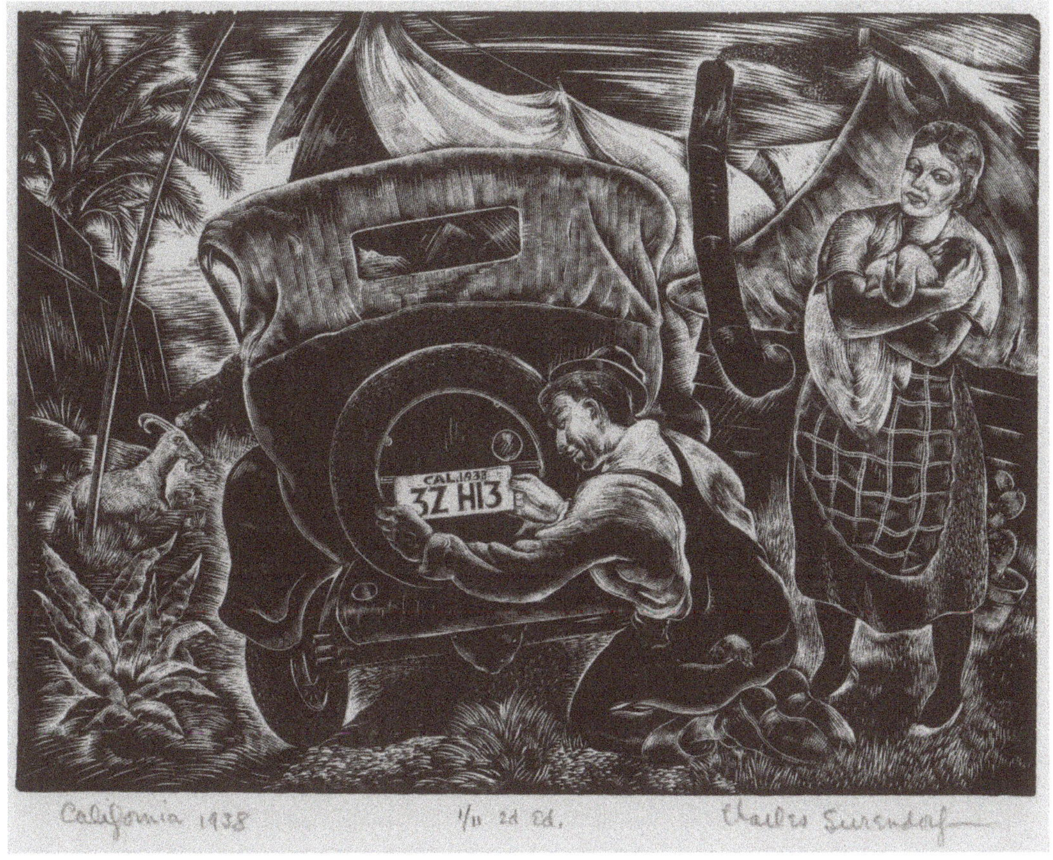

1938 California, **6×8 (1938).**

The writer John Steinbeck had friends in Surendorf's San Francisco neighborhood who owned some of his prints. Steinbeck was looking for an illustrator for a story he was working on and offered Surendorf the job. Unfortunately, Steinbeck's publisher had staff artists. When Steinbeck had to apologize for retracting the offer, Surendorf said, "He was mad as hell."

8: A Pacific Island Idyll

When Joan Brambila ended her romantic relationship with Surendorf, a new woman, Ethel Noland, entered his life. A divorcee with a Model A Ford roadster, Ethel didn't know how to drive, so Surendorf became her driver. When he shared with her his desire to go to Tahiti, she invited herself along and paid her own way. Plans were made to sail in January 1939 on a circuitous route that went to the island nation of Fiji first. Surendorf had to quit his job with the Federal Arts Project and sublet his apartment. He and Ethel took a train north to Vancouver, Canada, to board the ocean liner. In Honolulu they were supposed to connect with a twelve-passenger freighter to Suva, Fiji, then sail on to Tahiti. That boat was delayed two weeks.

Surendorf had to admit to his traveling companion that he was broke. He'd arrived with $3 in his pocket, and had counted on selling paintings and prints he'd brought with him to pay his expenses. Ethel went to look for a boarding house, and Surendorf completed three watercolors. He sold them immediately and had spending money from then on. He was grateful his companion was better financially prepared for the trip than he.

On a boat to Tahiti, Surendorf sold three watercolors he'd done during his stay in Fiji while on nature excursions there. "Those two weeks had been a pleasant unplanned experience. Possibly the most consistent span of pure enjoyment in my life," he said.

The sale of watercolors to meet expenses set them up for the rest of the trip. He and Ethel lived on Tahiti where, each month, twelve people arrived on a freighter and twelve departed. The mail came once a month. On the island,

Charles made the acquaintance of James Hall, coauthor of the book *Mutiny on the Bounty.* Hall told him, "Unpack your painting gear tomorrow and start painting. If you wait three days or a week you are lost."

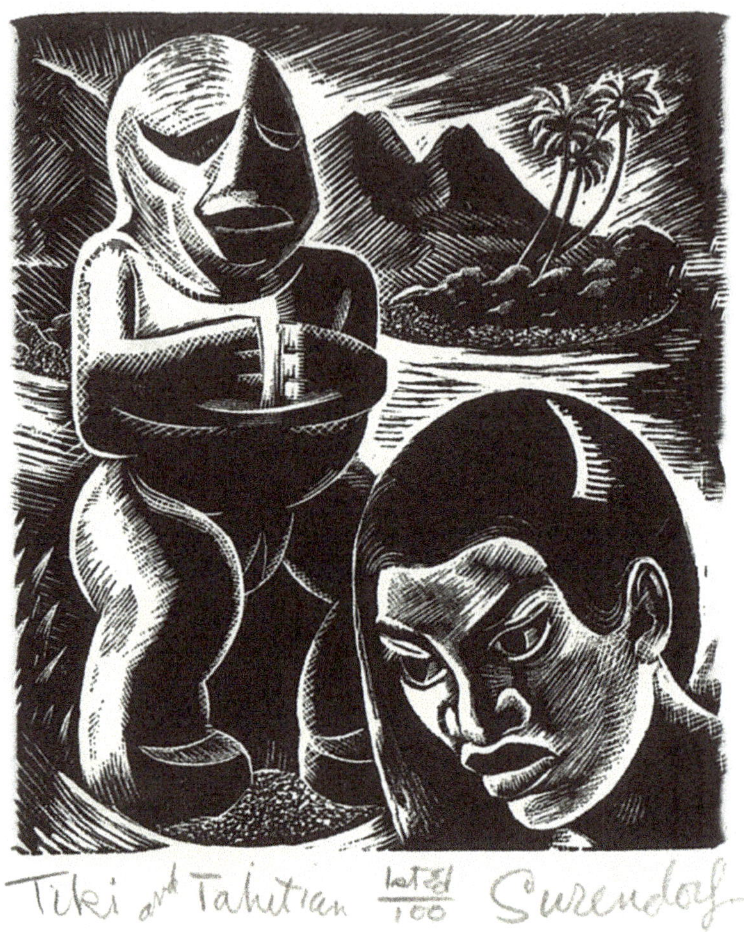

Tiki and Tahitian, **Tahiti, 3.75×3 (1939).**

Three miles from Papeete, Surendorf and Ethel found housing for $25 a month. There was a small English-speaking population. "Life was just too easy on the island. It could numb any desire to work," he recalled, so he got to work. He drank at the same bar the artist Paul Gauguin had frequented. Gauguin had run up enormous bar bills, but paid the bartenders in paintings. With a bicycle for

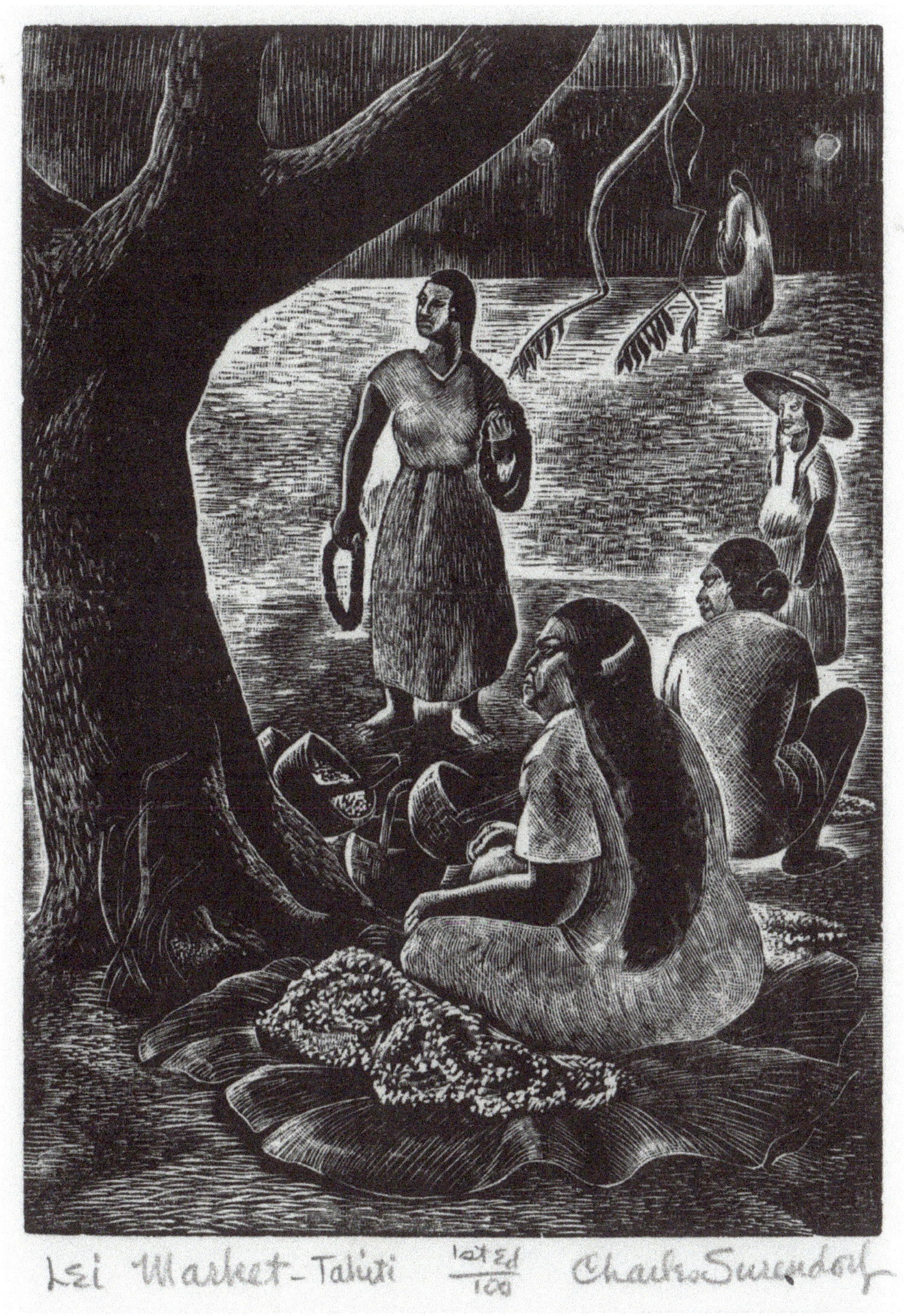

Lei Market, **Tahiti, 5×7 (1939).**

transportation, Surendorf pedaled off to paint and sketch. "Automatically the painting feelers darted here and there and the mind quickly composed the possible picture until something said, *This is it!* Then you paint," he said. On this first trip to Tahiti, Surendorf drew people, not scenery.

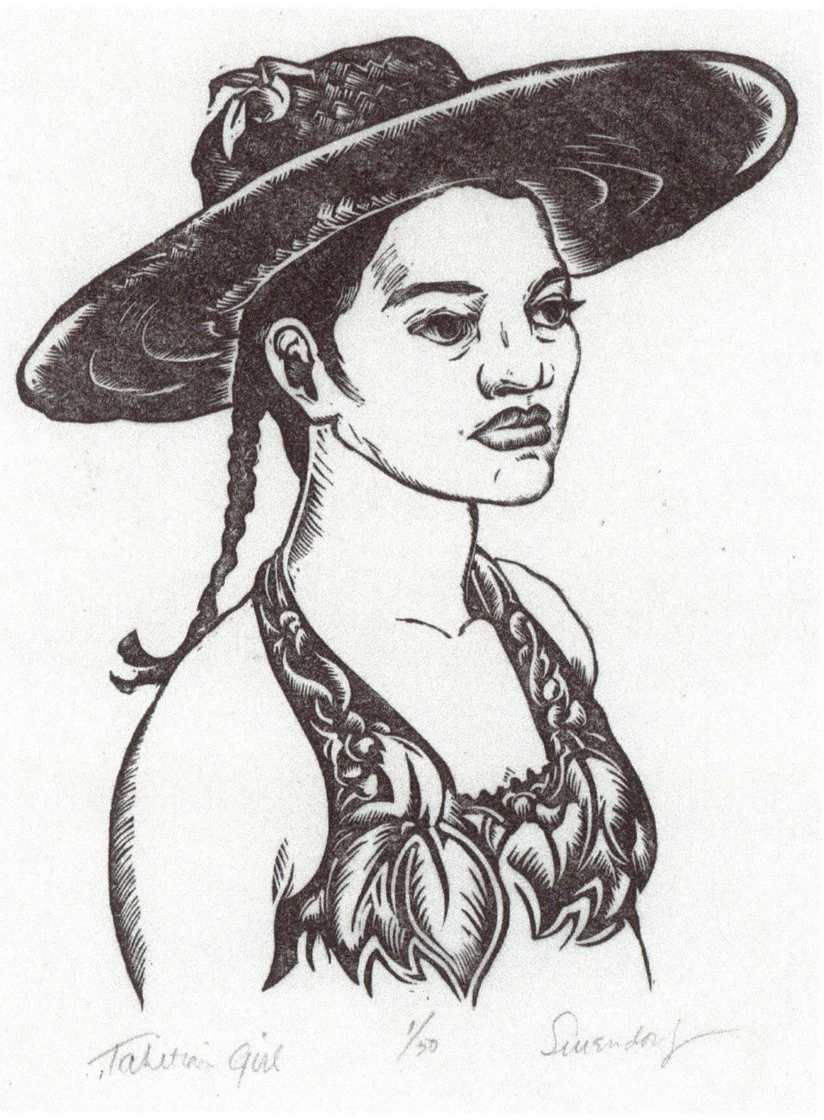

Tahitian Girl, Tahiti, 6×10 (1939).

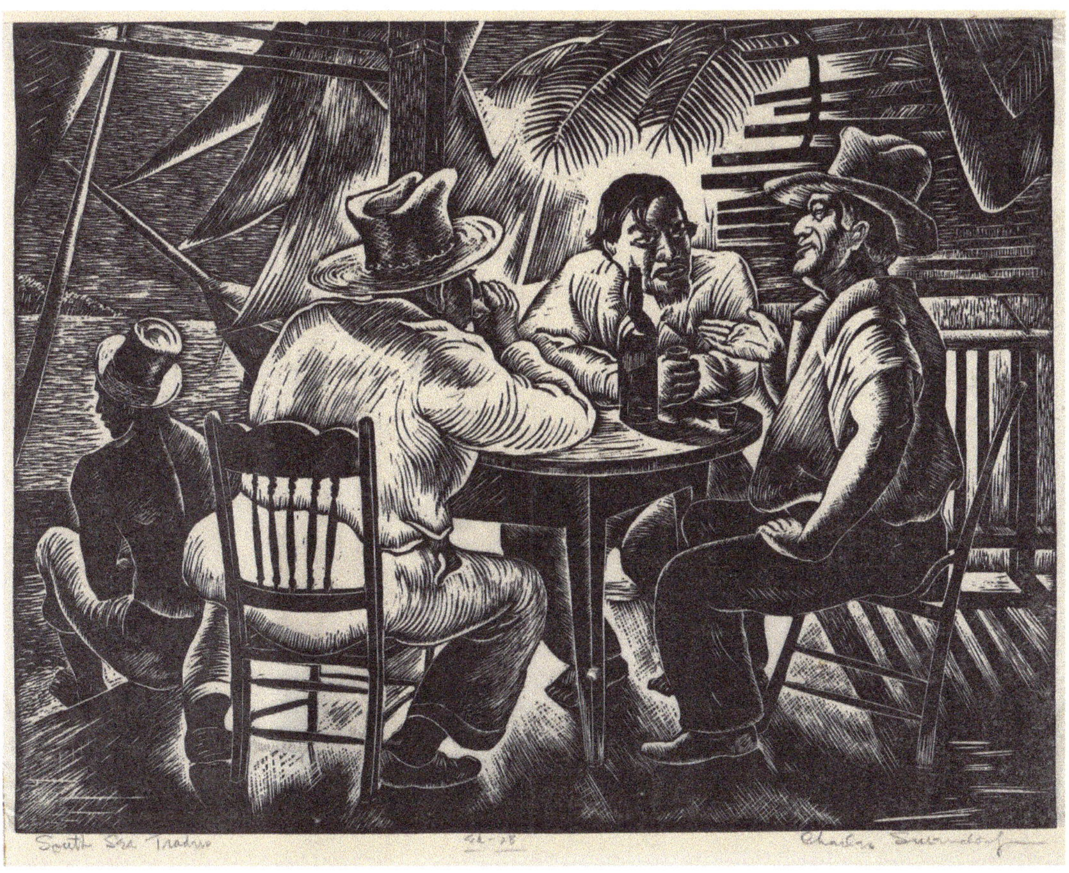

South Sea Traders, **Tahiti, 11×14 (1939).**

Having been forewarned, Surendorf wasn't surprised that Papeete was not the paradise of the South Pacific glamorized by tourist agencies. It held dilapidated wooden shacks and concrete buildings with sheet-metal roofs, but the natural world entranced him, from colored fish swimming among the boats in the harbor to the coral reefs the boats sailed over. Life was so easy on the island it could numb any desire to work, but he managed daily painting excursions with stops to swim nude with native girls in cool streams. He found Tahitian people kind and carefree, though very superstitious. The year in Tahiti flew by. Surendorf commented, "The sales of watercolors set the financial tone for the entire trip, so not again would I be hindered by money worries."

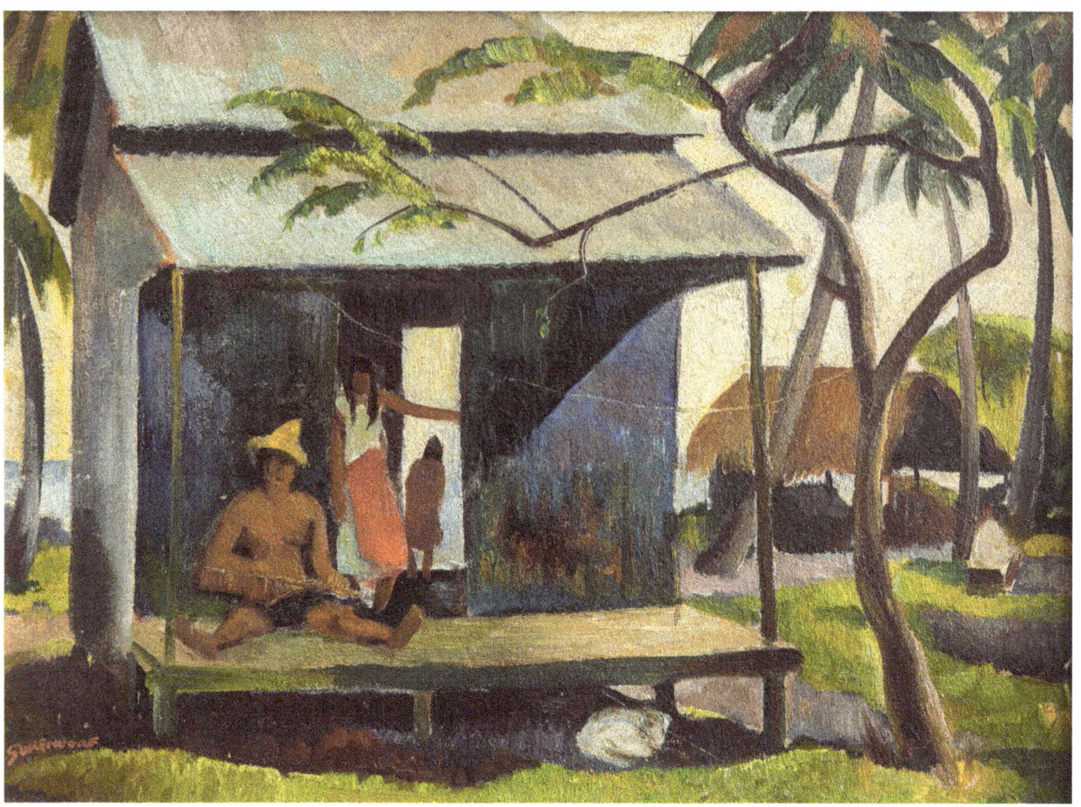

Tahitian Family Shack, **Tahiti, 12×16 (1940s).**

By the time they boarded the freighter to start the trip home, World War II had started. Arriving in San Francisco, Charles found his studio apartment was no longer available. His possessions awaited him in the basement and with luck he got his job with the Federal Arts Project back. What he lost was Ethel—she was ready to move on without him. The two friends would each seek their own original freedom and considered Tahiti a long lovely and romantic interlude.

Surendorf was eager to start engraving wood and linoleum blocks from his Tahiti sketches. "The work is a pleasurable way of passing an active day, as it can be started and stopped upon will without disrupting the continuity of the press." He compared the work to a long treasure hunt; the effort is consummated when the proof (print) is made and the reward revealed. "Then, with the final finished block, unlimited prints can be made and enjoyed by hundreds of owners rather than just a few, as is the case with a privately owned painting."

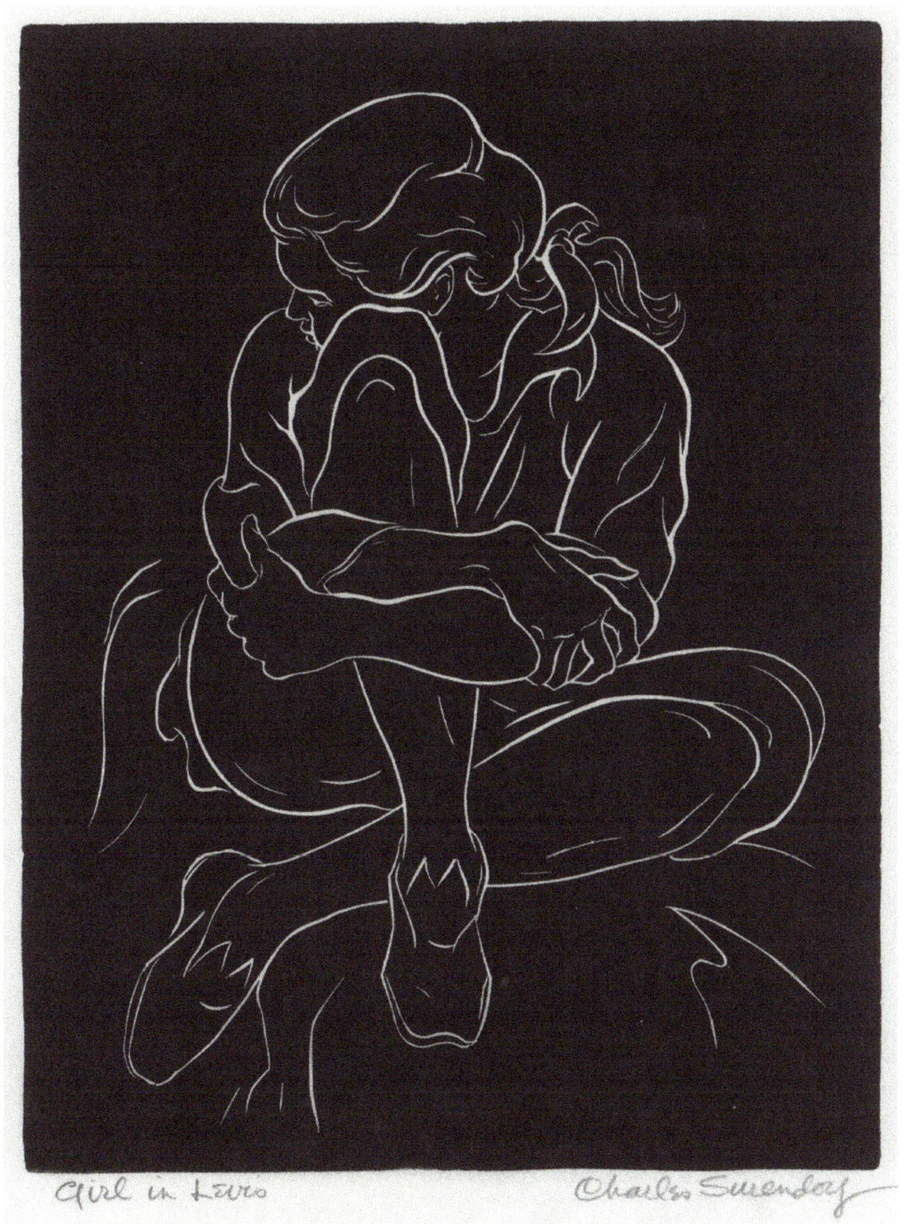

Girl in Levis, **8×11 (1940s).**

After finding new temporary housing, Charles spent lots of time at the Montgomery Block, an imposing four-story pre-earthquake San Francisco building. Homes and studios rented at $10 a month, and the building featured two bistros. He had heard

William Saroyan was a frequent visitor to the Montgomery Block, home to the famous bohemians of the time. He asked a friend at a bistro for an introduction. The man said, "Charlie, you shouldn't be putting those straight whiskies away so fast. You sat across the table from Saroyan for three hours last night."

Surendorf recalled:

Often my memory serves me not so well when recalling a bistro binge. Somehow much of the drinking pleasure becomes lost and it becomes necessary to make light of the unaccounted time as part of the price paid for other alcoholic emotions. Up to a certain degree of drunkenness it is possible to pace drinks, an ounce an hour with the aid of a clock, but control soon disintegrates. This lamentable limbo, along with the inevitable hangover, eventually becomes the acceptable standard of a drinker's philosophy. I was dedicated to my work, and only when a project was successfully completed would I allow myself time out for booze. This fact and the chronic state of my financial depression were the two main factors in control of my drinking.

Often at this vital point I feel a nervous, restless, churning desire that leaves my body visibly shaken, although inwardly there is a feeling of binding tenseness. There is undoubtably a satanic force urging the urge. It can only be alleviated or destroyed by a furious action—painting, writing, working in the yard, or chopping wood. Cooking and eating vast quantities of a favorite food is also a workable deterrent. When one makes a habit of drinking this can become a daily or, at the best, a weekly battle.

When I did not take it out on a bottle I managed to saturate myself with sex. It was easy—as unrestrictive as ordering a shot of bourbon. I was fairly young, about thirty-five, tanned and well known in the art circles of the city. The ease of the conquests astonished me. Combining booze soon was the order of the day and the game was a different woman every night. Yet, with all my successful nocturnal indulgences there was an emptiness. The flashes of bright chalk on the blackboard were but bursts of transitory color.

In an attempt to link the arts community to the social elite of San Francisco, the Junior League, a debutantes' group, invited recognized artists to paint their portraits. These finished pieces of art would be displayed at a grand dance. Artists might or might not be paid commissions for the portraits. Some had no skills when it came to portrait painting. Surendorf's picture of Sheila Peart and her poodle, painted in 1941, was good work.

When newspaper praise came his way, Surendorf clipped it and saved it, such as this *Indianapolis Star* story from May 4, 1941:

> There are few artists, those gifted with a "divine spark of genius," who can do things without knowing why. Charles Surendorf can make a good picture… he has a remarkable gift of imagination. His print from Tahiti, *Sidewalk Café*, shows technical elegance.

A fellow Federal Arts Project artist introduced Charles to a blond social worker from Atascadero, California. Ten years his junior, she was a UC Berkeley graduate named Natalia Payne. Charles quickly fell in love with her and proposed marriage. He felt there had to be a logical basis for the whirlwind engagement. They'd met at the right time and the right place, and in conversation, ideas and ideals were exchanged and found compatible. Two weeks after they'd met, a quick trip to Nevada made them husband and wife.

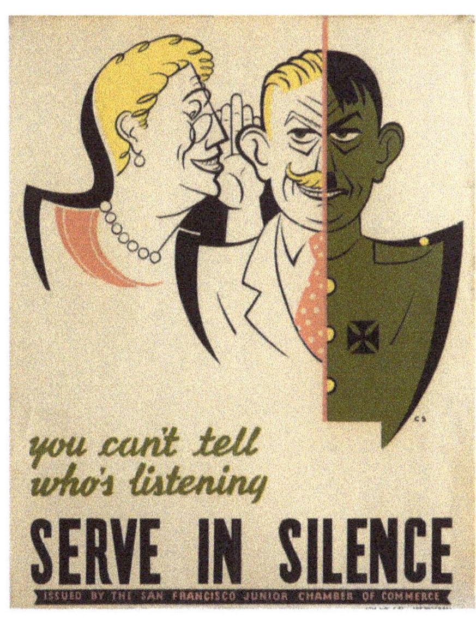

FAP War Effort Poster, **WWII, 17×22 (1940s).**

The Federal Arts Project folded with America's entrance into World War II. Surendorf registered for the draft and got a job in a shipyard, manufacturing aluminum lifeboats for the navy. He worried about being drafted. "I knew I would make a damn poor soldier; artists usually do; we are temperamentally disinclined to be commanded." A pre-induction medical exam, however, indicated a chance of hypertension, and Charles was classified 1B and temporarily deferred military service. He switched jobs, went to work for Bethlehem Steel, and his skill in typing got him a job as a night office manager. He took nighttime naps at work and painted during the day.

Baby Tamara Karla was born in October 1942. The regular arrival of regular paychecks was a great relief after the long Depression years, and Charles's prints were selling well in local galleries. Sometimes an anticipated move gave inspiration to a block print. Surendorf carved a block with three people on a sidewalk at the bottom of a flight of exterior stairs—it was Charles and Natalia holding Karla, surrounded by possessions, their belligerent landlady at the top of the stairs shaking her finger at them. The print, called *Eviction*, had Surendorf's emotions carved into it. The *San Francisco Chronicle* printed it in an article on the lack of housing in the city during the post-war years.

The family bought a small house, and Natalia went back to work for the Florence Crittenton Home for Unwed Mothers. She brought home a good salary while Surendorf made art and practiced self-promotion. Gump's department store held a show of his Mother Lode prints and paintings in their gallery. The prints garnered prizes in graphic arts shows nationwide.

"I attributed it all to the fact that I had gone completely on the wagon and stayed on the wagon for twenty years… it was the dullest period of my life. It is perfectly natural for an alcoholic to view a long siege of sobriety with that perspective." His sobriety was an attempt to save his marriage, but it didn't work—Natalia left him. "The four years of

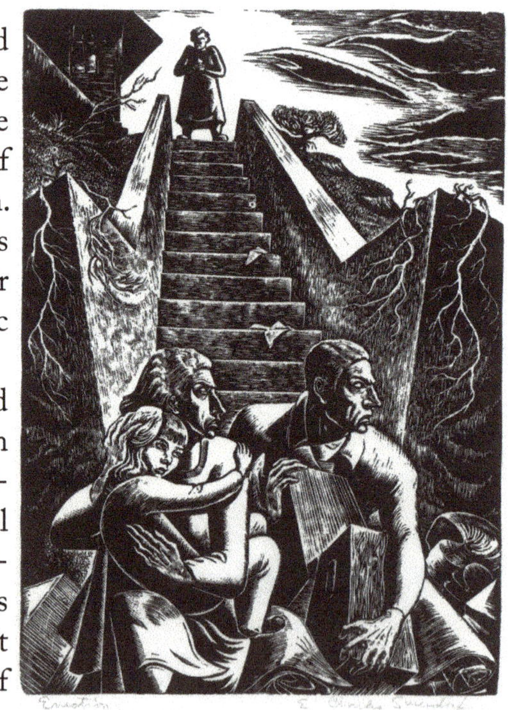

Eviction, San Francisco, 8×12 (1940s).

marriage had, with all the drinking, molded me into the groove of a father and a responsible husband," Surendorf mused.

Times were busy: The City of San Francisco Committee for Municipal Art (now the San Francisco Arts Commission) elected Surendorf their first director for a planned outdoor art festival in 1946; 250,000 people attended. Stanford University paid him a $500 fee to organize an art show there. Also, he illustrated a children's book, *Mr. Pimney,* for author Justus Edwin Wyman. The book featured seventeen woodcuts about a ghost who didn't know how to haunt. It was Surendorf's only children's book.

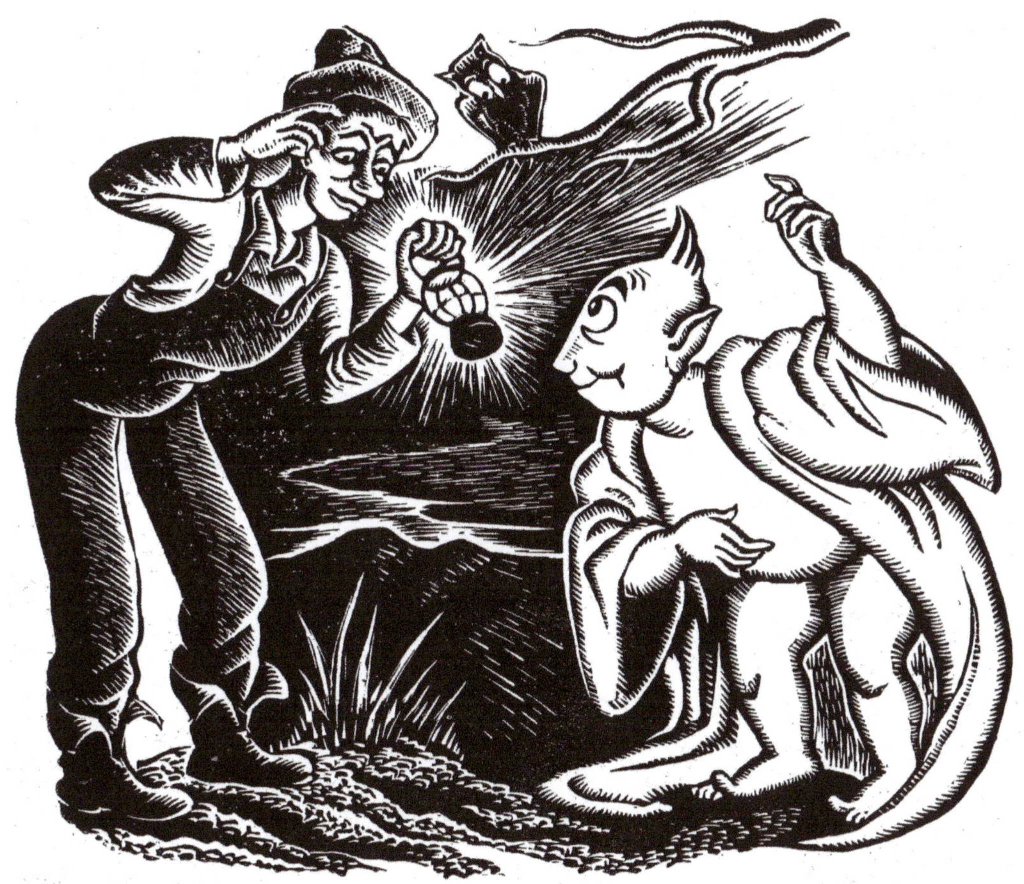

A Woodcut from **"Mr. Pimney."**

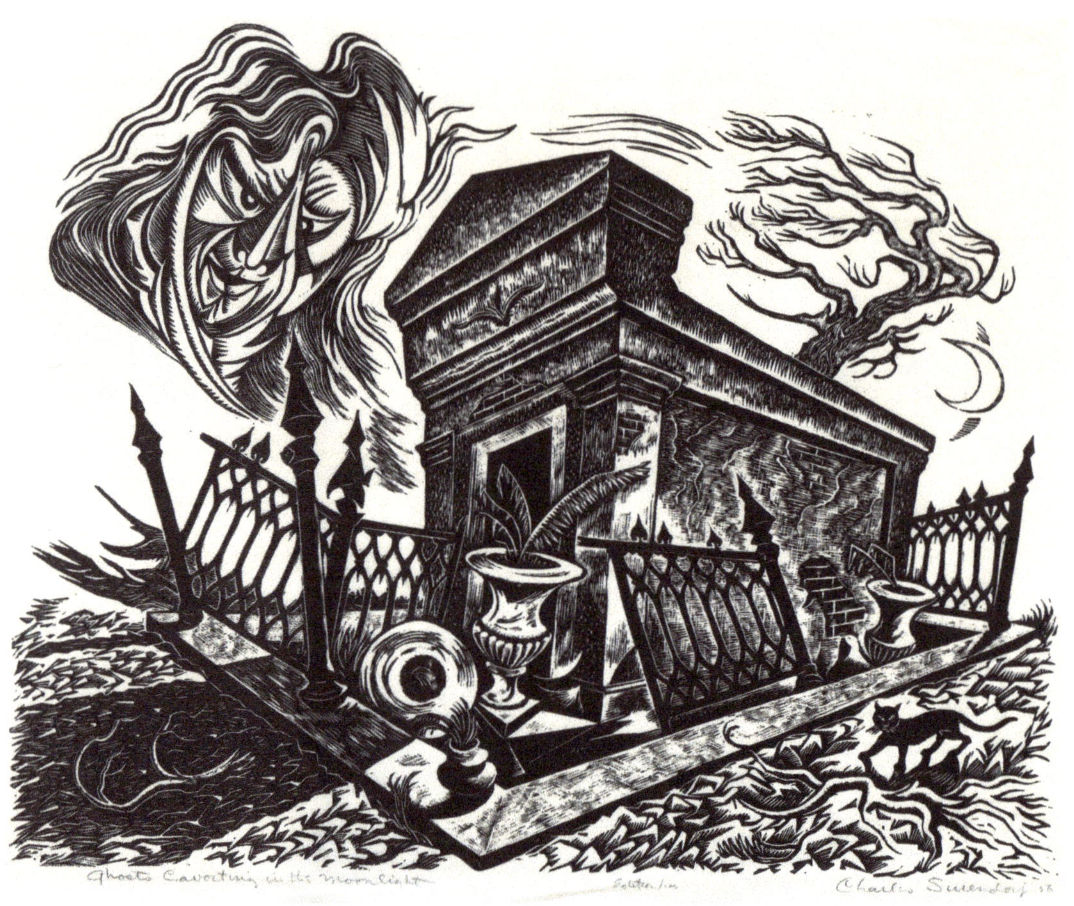

Ghosts Cavorting, New Orleans, 12×16 (1956).

Surendorf's mother had passed away in Indiana, and Charles wanted to take Karla back to meet his dad, but first he had to raise the money to pay for a Pullman sleeping berth on the train. Ever creative, he noticed an empty shop next to, and owned by, the Western Pacific Railroad ticket office on Post Street across from Gump's. He got them to donate the space for a show and had his journalist friend, Herb Caen, publicize it. By Christmas 1946 he had the funds for the trip back east.

Ready to leave the big city and settle in Columbia, he found temporary housing with a room to use as a studio/gallery, and, with a fellow artist, began to plan the art school they wanted to establish. A large hotel in nearby Sonora covered its walls with his paintings and prints, and Surendorf started to make good sales from there.

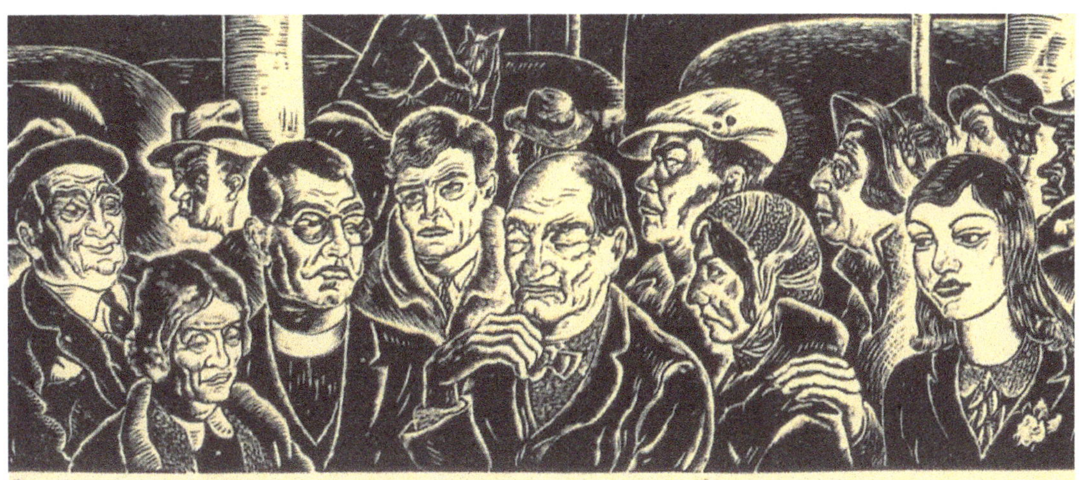

The President Speaks, **wood engraving 16×23 (ca. 1934–1943)**

Having no car, Charles hitchhiked everywhere. He soon found a building on Columbia's main street where, for $15 a month, he rented the backroom, complete with toilet and washbasin, and a studio/gallery in front. Now he could live and work in the center of town. He traded his prints for used furniture for his living space. A block print of St. Anne's Church was his first sale at $5. Surendorf made money buying art supplies wholesale and then selling them at a profit to his prospective art students. Settled in at Columbia, he was ready for a new adventure—a trip to New Orleans.

Chapter 9: The Big Easy

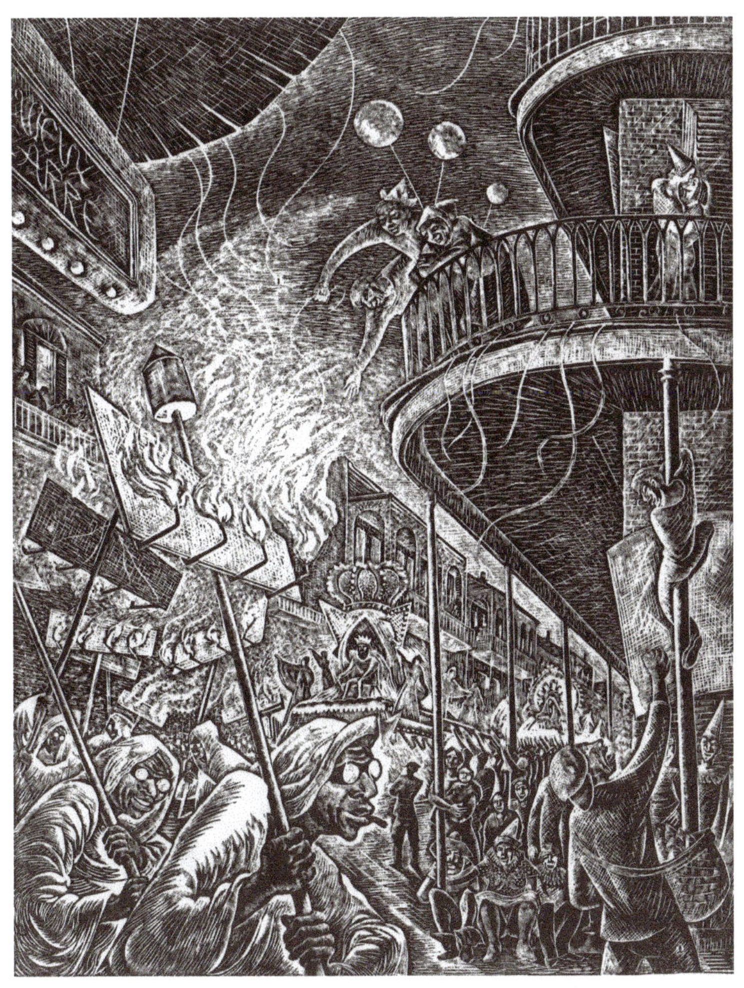

Mardi Gras, **New Orleans, 12×17.75 (1949).**

On arriving in New Orleans, Charles rented a room on the corner of St. Peter and Royal streets. He blended in with the art community and sold just enough pieces to keep him in paint, food, and booze. He traded prints, a custom among printmakers, indicative of mutual admiration. Surendorf felt the French Quarter had an intangible art feeling found in few places in the world.

Remembering the advice from his South Seas trip, he made his first sketch a balcony scene looking down St. Peter Street. He believed every inch of the French Quarter offered endless composition and exuded the mystic aura of age. He avidly sketched compositions for future block prints.

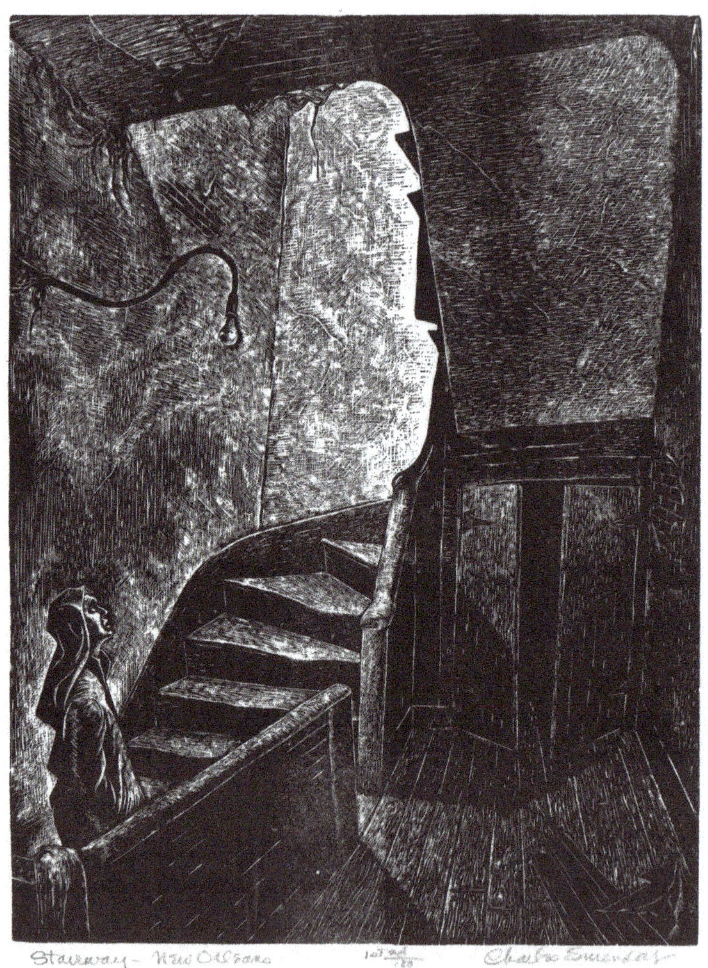

Stairway, **New Orleans, 13.75×10 (1949).**

In later years, Surendorf always wondered why there was a greater demand for his New Orleans prints in Columbia than in the French Quarter itself. A French restaurant, Vieux Carré, in Palo Alto, California, filled its walls with his New Orleans paintings.

Returning to California, Surendorf discovered that some Columbia residents were trying to encourage the California State Park system to buy the whole town for a display of what the Gold Rush environment had looked like. The plan would be to restore the ancient structures to their original design and strength. In 1945, Governor Earl Warren approved the idea, and lot by lot the state acquired four blocks of Main Street and one block of each of four side streets. Businesses and private homes would be restored and then rented for commercial use.

This process eliminated the rental rooms available to the summer art students at Charles's Mother Lode Art School. A movie crew turned up to film *Artists of the Mother Lode,* and Surendorf demonstrated painting and running off a block print in his studio space. The film was shown in San Francisco public schools, and more than once over the years the children of visiting tourists would proclaim, "I saw you in a movie!"

Accepting an etching job at the College of Arts and Crafts in Berkeley in 1947, Charles commuted from Sonora to the Bay Area on a Greyhound bus. Co-ed girls who owned cars gave him rides back up to Columbia and then spend the weekend sketching and entertaining their teacher. Older instructors warned Surendorf about amorous relationships with students.

Near the end of that first fall semester Charles was asked to chaperone a school dance. To liven things up he got the girls to put on lipstick and plant big kiss imprints all over his face. Administrators ordered him to leave the dance, which he did, but he also called in the story about his caper to Herb Caen at the *Chronicle.* The stunt cost Charles his teaching job, as the college promptly fired him.

Finding Columbia deserted again in winter, he decided to return to New Orleans. His paintings, watercolors, and prints were selling better than he'd expected, so he took a train to Louisiana and rented the same room he'd had before. French Quarter art dealers were happy with his prints, but after only a month Columbia was dominating his thoughts, so he headed back west again. When it's hardened by cold temperatures, linoleum engraves like wood, so Charles quickly turned his New Orleans adventure into engraved blocks for printing upon his return to the Sierra foothills.

A trip to San Francisco found Surendorf at his favorite Chinese restaurant. At the next table was a woman he recognized as working in the City of Paris department store's Rotunda Art Gallery. Being what he referred to as "woman-starved" at that point in his life, he introduced himself to Barbara Stoner. Enchanted with the lovely assistant art curator for the gallery, within a week he wanted to marry her. She was quite taken with Charles, and he took her to Peter Macchiarini's jewelry shop on Grant Avenue to see a gold band he'd had made for her, studded with tiny gold nuggets. Barbara said yes to his marriage proposal.

Judge Muese, the justice of the peace in Columbia, performed the wedding ceremony. Surendorf's neighbors gathered as witnesses, but Lito Collins, the best man, was missing—with the wedding ring. Hours of searching ensued until Lito was found sound asleep in the back of the judge's darkened chambers. That night an old miners' custom, a shivaree, took place. On their first night in bed, the newlyweds were harassed with gravel grating on the windows and hooting and hollering outside.

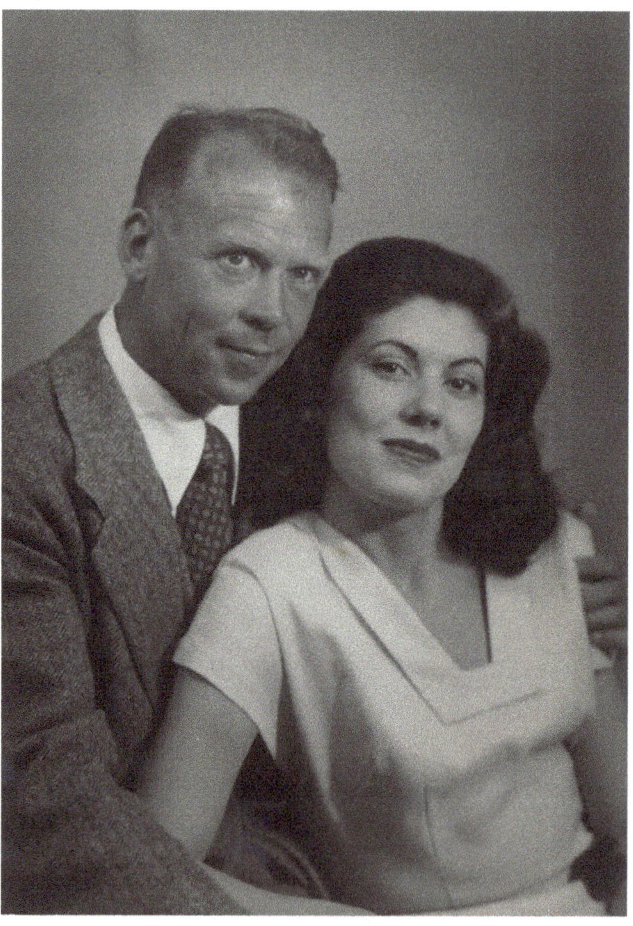

Happy Newlyweds, **4.5×6.5 (1940s).**

Living in a small room in the back of their gallery and studio, the new Mrs. Surendorf settled into the spirit of Columbia. She and her husband liked to sunbathe on the plank sidewalk outside the studio. Surendorf noted, "She did not mind the constant stream of inquisitive locals that peeked around the corner of the building to watch a beautiful dame in a scantily tailored swimsuit sitting on the edge of the street."

During the late 1940s, Surendorf established the Mother Lode Art School as a way to increase income. Groups of students traveled from the Bay Area to the ghost town for lessons in composition, mixing colors, and general techniques. The school came to an end when Barbara expressed jealousy over Charles's close relationships with several female art students; a lack of rooms to rent due to the restorations didn't help either.

In 1949 the town of Columbia hoped to be part of a statewide celebration of California's centennial and the Gold Rush. A week of pageants and demonstrations occurred in 100-degree heat. Though the state provided little advance publicity, it expected enormous crowds, and made visitors park a mile away and walk into town. Local merchants lost money because the state allowed a cheap carnival to set up on the edge of town. The original Pay-Ore Saloon next to Surendorf's gallery was recreated and staffed for the event, but the throngs never arrived. Charles set up an outdoor art show only to have several oils, watercolors, and prints stolen. The complete flop of the centennial celebration made the nation's newspapers, but it was undesirable publicity.

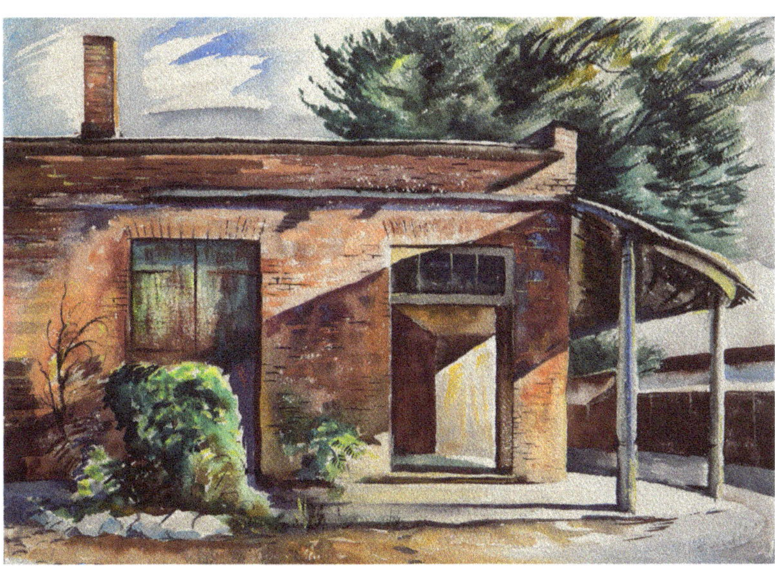

Pay Ore Corner, **Columbia, 20.5×15 (1960s).**

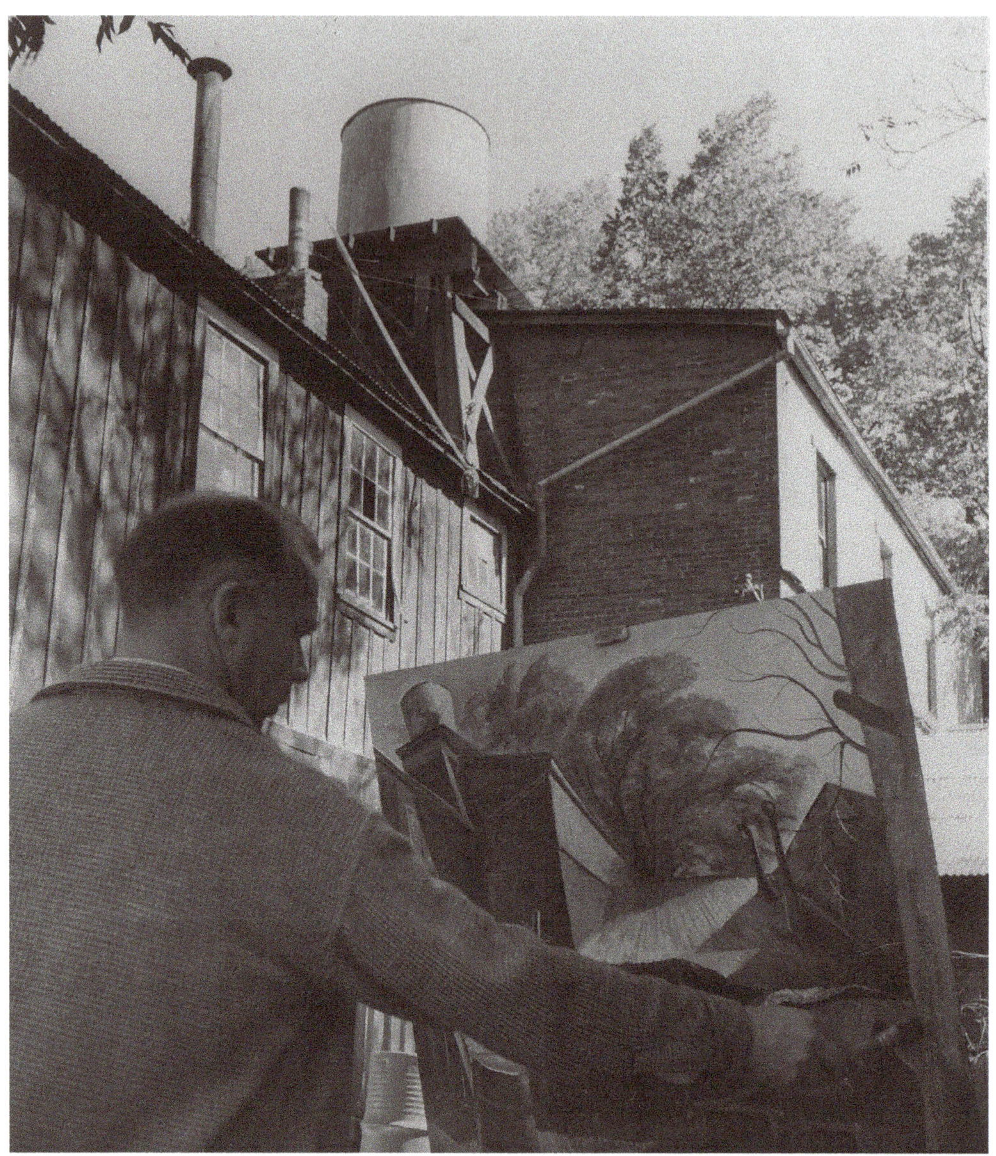

Artist Painting Ruins Outdoors, **Columbia, 8×10 (1960s).**

Surendorf and a new resident state park ranger clashed on everything about Columbia, from dogs loose on the streets to the use of garbage cans. The ranger approved razing buildings he referred to as "a pile of junk," and the old livery stables disappeared as did other old buildings. A lovely area of lush vegetation covering old rocky diggings was bulldozed and paved to become a huge parking lot.

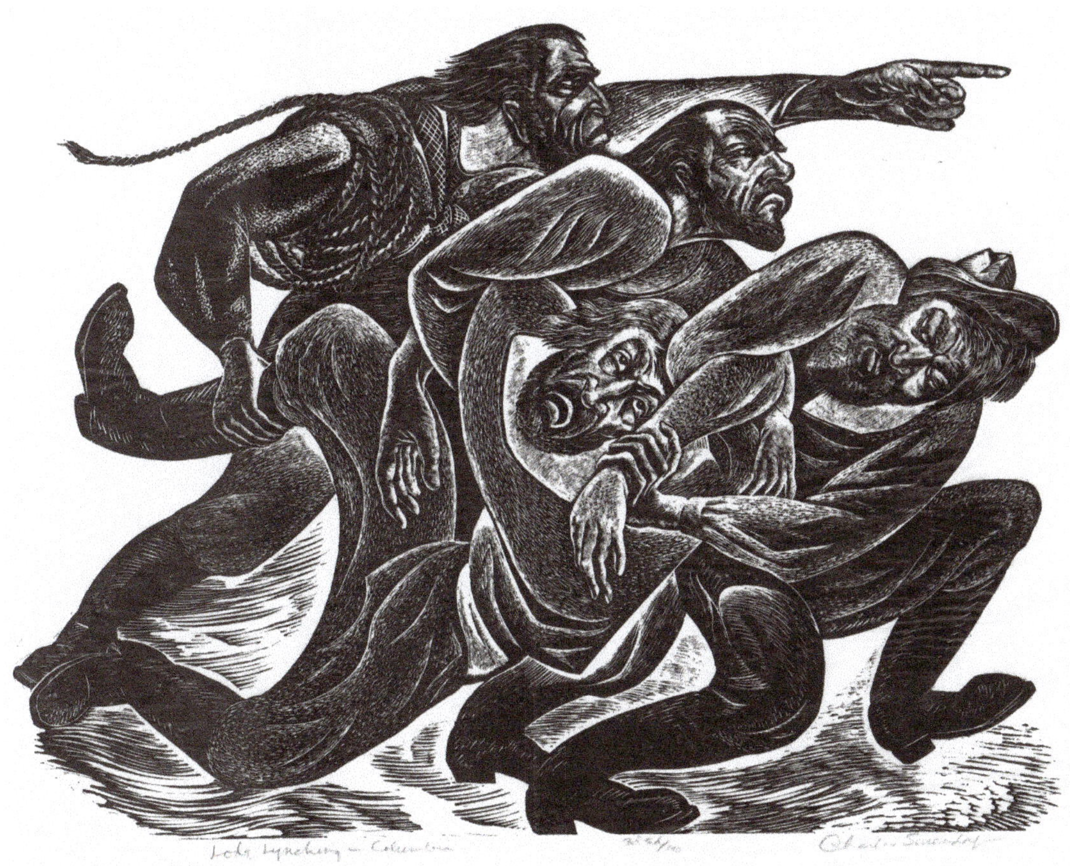

Lode Lynching, **Columbia, 10×16 (1950s).**

Combining practicality and publicity, Surendorf obtained a Chevrolet sedan delivery van and painted MOTHER LODE ART GALLERY and SURENDORF STUDIO on the sides. On trips to San Francisco, this allowed him to park in yellow curb zones and not be ticketed.

With a comfortable bed installed in the vehicle, and a supply of prints to sell, Charles and his wife, now pregnant with their first child, locked up the Columbia studio and took off for an adventure. They would go to New Orleans, tour the South, then go to the Midwest and visit family. Barbara informed Charles that she was unhappy with their marriage and was considering leaving him and staying with her family.

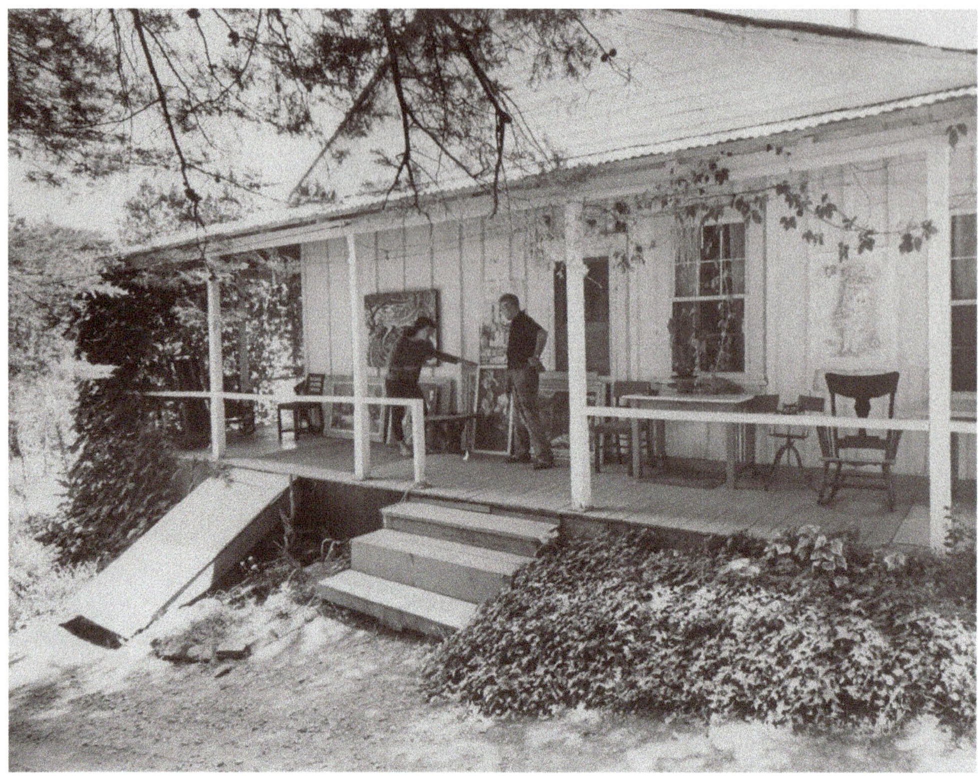

Mother Lode Art Gallery, **Columbia, 8×10 (1960s).**

On reaching New Orleans, they found temporary quarters with living space in a backroom and exhibition space in the front. Barbara monitored the gallery while Surendorf spent every available hour painting enough pieces to have the one-man show of New Orleans watercolors that he hoped for. Their idea for a tiny gallery was a financial flop.

They traveled to Florida and Georgia to visit with relatives. Then, arriving in Indiana, they visited Charles's old friend, Roy Hirshburg, in his hometown of Richmond. Roy showed Barbara the town of Logansport, Indiana, where his painting career had begun. They next visited Surendorf's dad, and then went to Goshen, where Barbara's parents lived. After that visit, Barbara no longer felt any desire to remain in the Midwest.

Surendorf noted, "With the ice and the snow and the cold of an Indiana winter, watercolors were impossible to paint. The pigment froze before I could get it on the paper. I was forced to paint in oils."

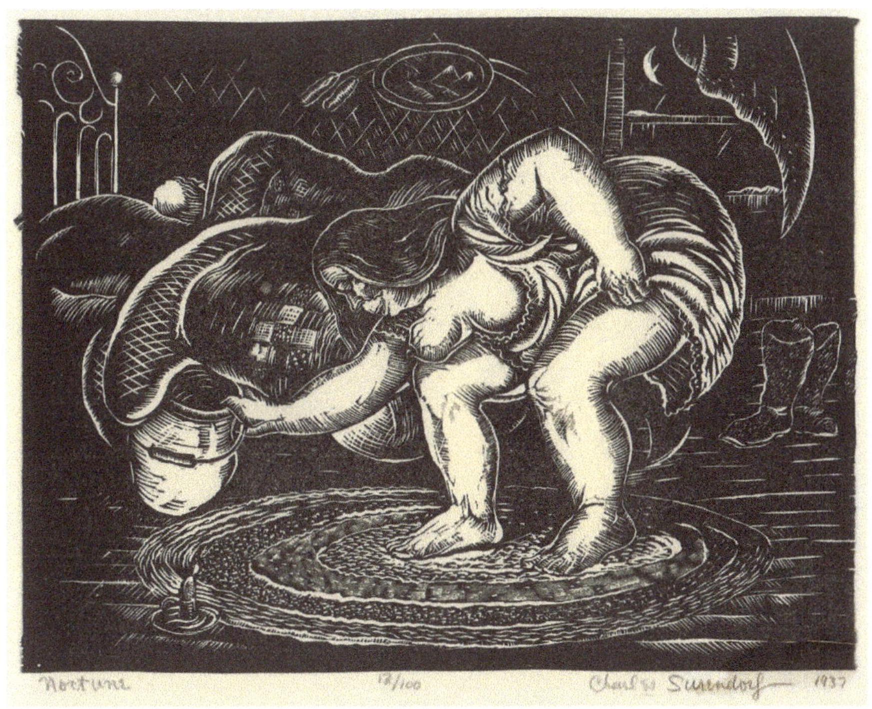

Nocturne, **8×10 (1940s).**

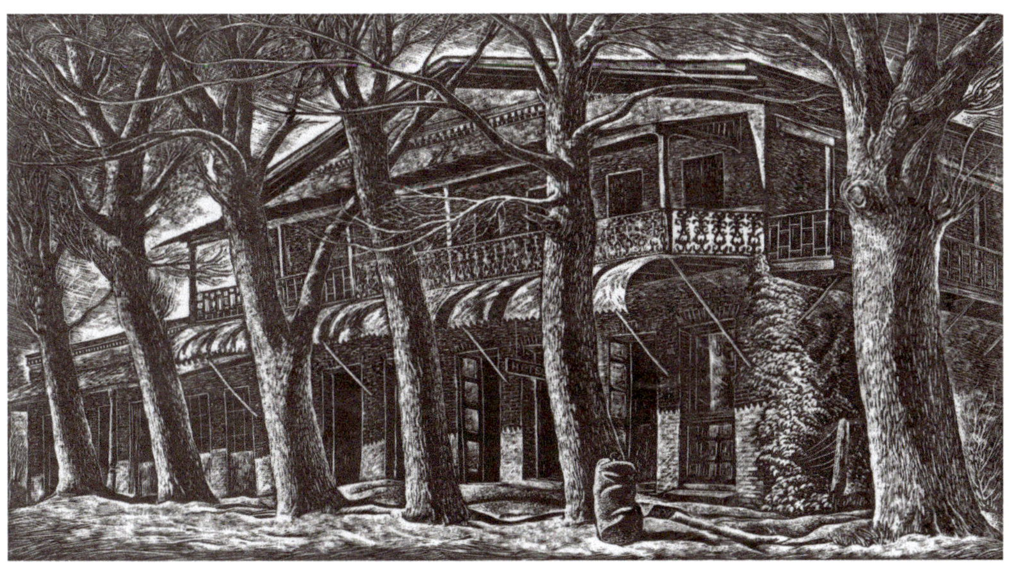

City Hotel, **Columbia, 8×10 (1950s)**

10: A Growing Family

Having had their fill of travel, the couple headed home to California. Aware that with a baby on the way they'd need a bigger living space, they used Columbia's gossip grapevine to find a four-room house on Yankee Hill, and on February 17, 1950, Charles Surendorf III arrived.

The winter's absence of tourists froze art sales in Columbia. The gallery's admission coinbox was empty, and Charles owed child-support payments to his first wife, Natalia, for Karla, and had to make car payments as well. Charles priced hundreds of prints with slightly soiled mats at $2 each, and from their sale he made enough to pay rent and buy food. In the nick of time a tourist bought a winter landscape oil painting, for which he paid enough to cover Karla's child support and the car payments for three months. Surendorf noted, "And not once since then have I ever encountered the awful sensation that comes from being dead broke."

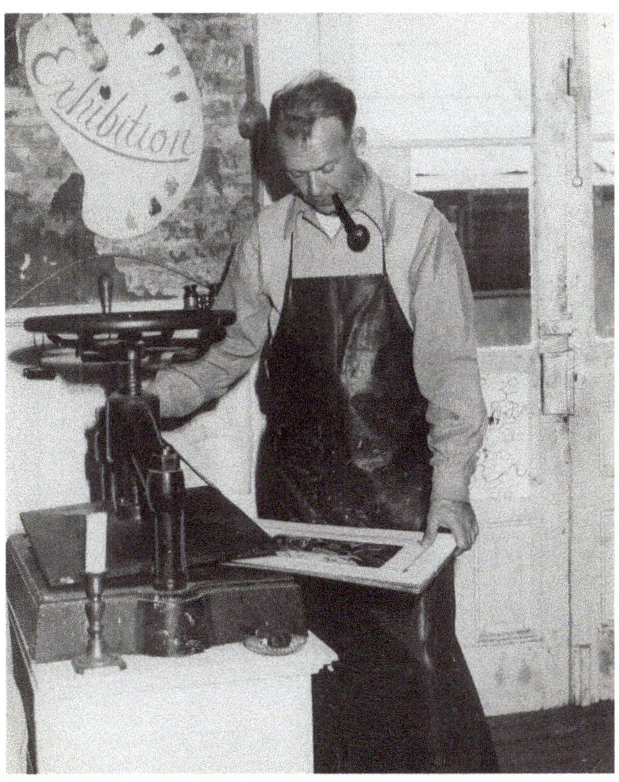

Printmaking, **Columbia, 8×10 (1960s).**

"Realizing I would soon need more income than just what was coming in on my block prints, I dickered with the landlord for the two empty buildings in front along Main Street," Surendorf recalled. "He let me have the largest for $15 a month extra. Finding myself with a vast array of walls, I was able to exhibit hundreds of oils and watercolors. The gallery was so large now that it was impossible to police, so rather than having a mob flowing through and no one to deter picture snatching, I converted a sturdy old communion stand into a collection box, narrowed the main entrance, and charged ten cents to enter."

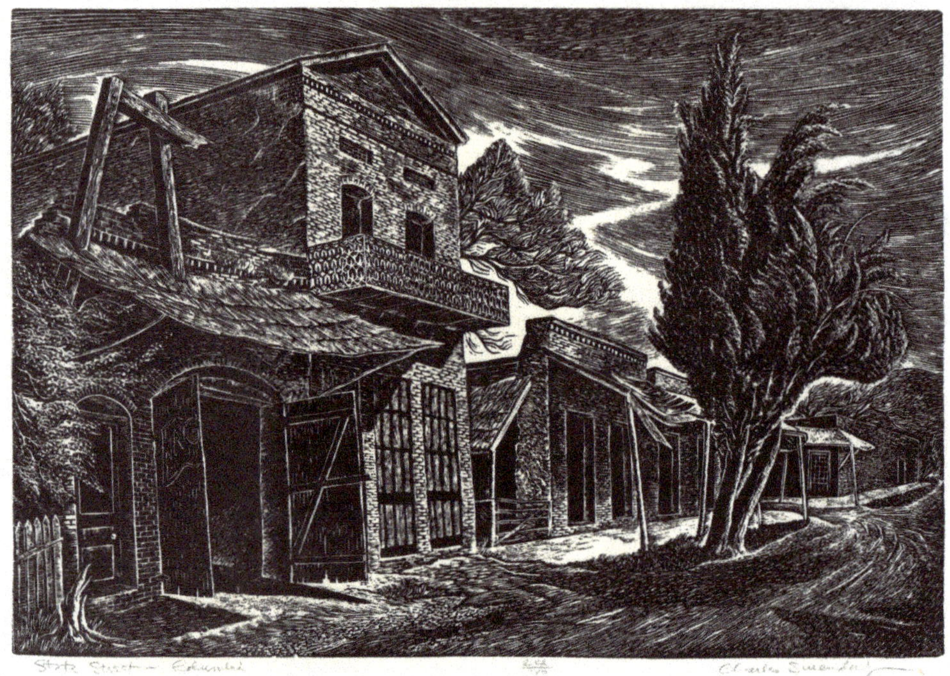

State (Main) Street, **Columbia, 8×10 (1950s).**

In July 1951, another new baby, Stephanie, arrived. The infant girl was born with a rare craniofacial cleft, widely separated eyes, and a spread nose. These issues made her eligible for State Crippled Children's Aid, and she had facial reconstruction and dental work done over a period of years.

On a brighter note, art sales were picking up; watercolors painted in the morning sold in the afternoon. Multiple sales happened every day. One day, a man showed up at the studio and bought $1,000 worth of oil paintings.

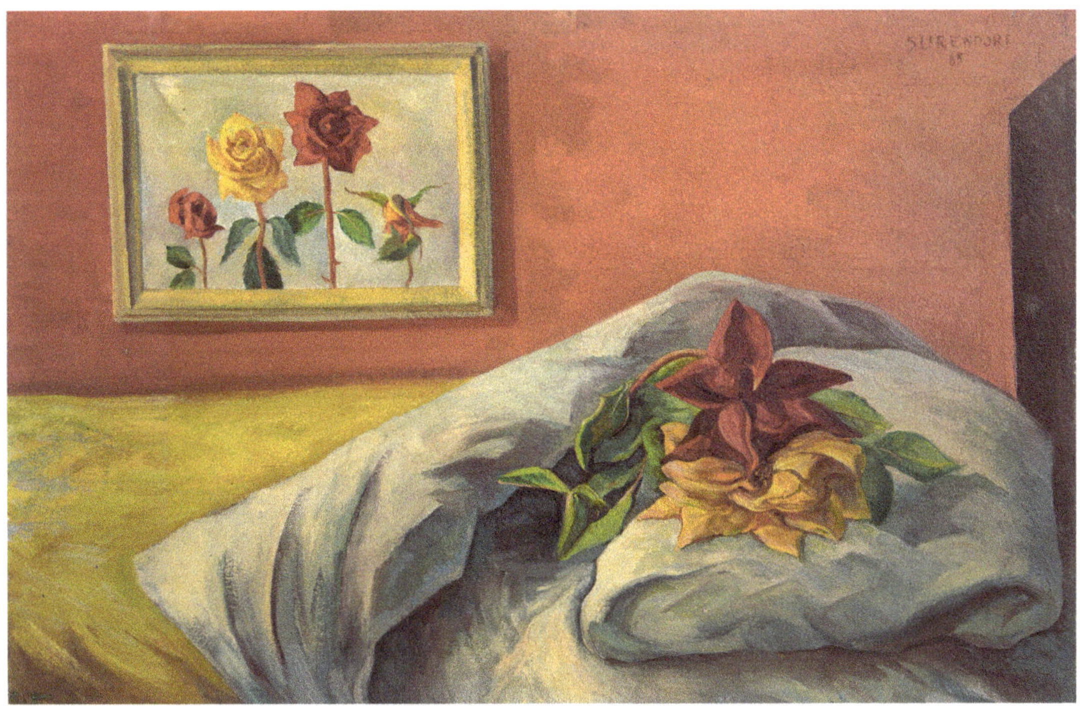

Bed of Roses, **36×24 (nd).**

At Christmas, the family took a quick trip back to Indiana to see family, and arrived back in Columbia in time to find a strange padlock on their gallery door. In the rush of leaving on their trip, Charles had accidentally left his gallery door unlocked. Friends in Columbia knew he was out of town so they put a lock on the building after seeing that it had been open for days.

Entering the gallery, a worried Surendorf found a pile of envelopes on his desk with money inside them for purchases. His petty cash box was undisturbed and his admission coinbox was stuffed full of coins. "My mistake in leaving the front door to the gallery opened nearly paid the expenses of the entire vacation," he said. Awaiting them on their return also was a notice that they had three months to find a new gallery space, as the state intended to restore their building.

In 1953, the growing Surendorf family needed more living space, and they found a wood-frame house on Kennebec Hill just outside the state park boundary. On twenty-six acres of land with an irrigation canal flowing through it, the vegetation around the house flourished. The parcel had fig trees, apples, pears, walnuts, and grapevines. At the top of the driveway was a cypress tree seven feet wide at its base. The rent on the ramshackle structure was $35 a month. Extensive remodeling and painting ensued. The landlord was so startled by the improvements that he raised the monthly rent to $45 because it was now a nicer place. The rent remained $45 for the next twenty years, and Surendorf would live there until the end of his life.

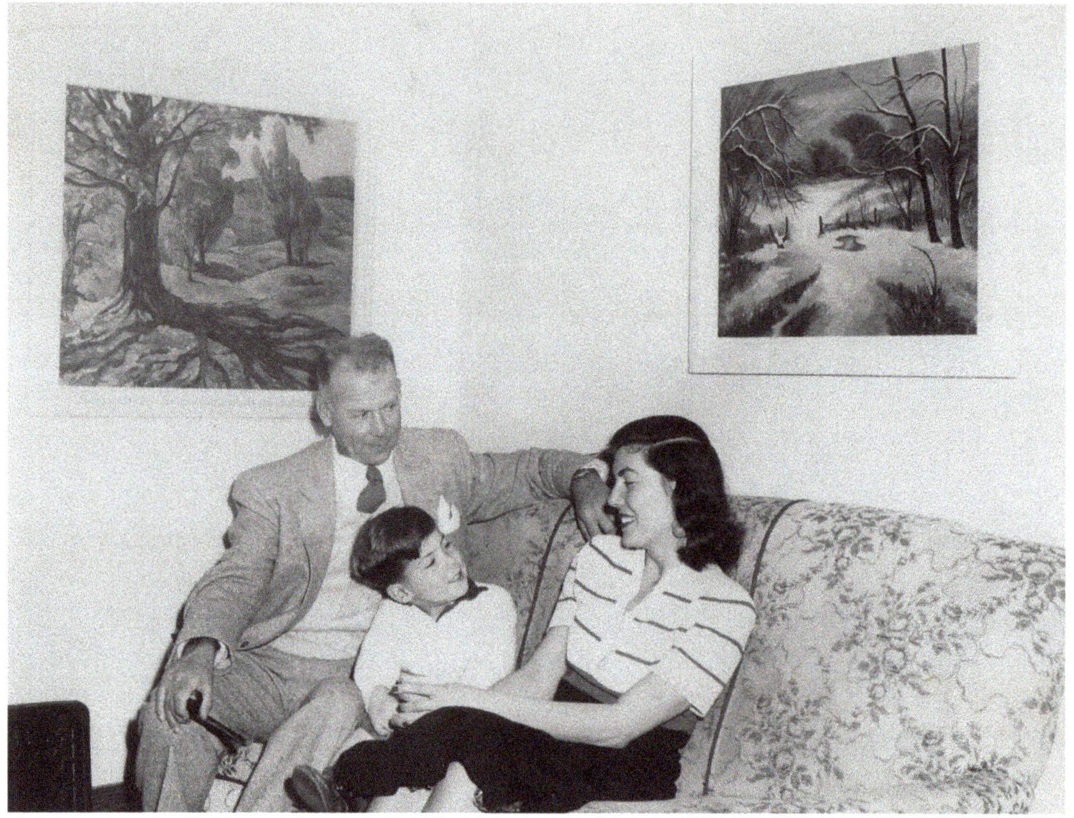

Family Portrait with Son, **Columbia, 8×10 (1950s).**

After the family had settled in, fellow artists began to visit. Emmy Lou Packard, whose block prints of the Mendocino Coast were as memorable as Surendorf's of Columbia, arrived from San Francisco. Charles Safford, the artist's old friend from Coachella, came year after year to paint and to discuss what was happening in the art world.

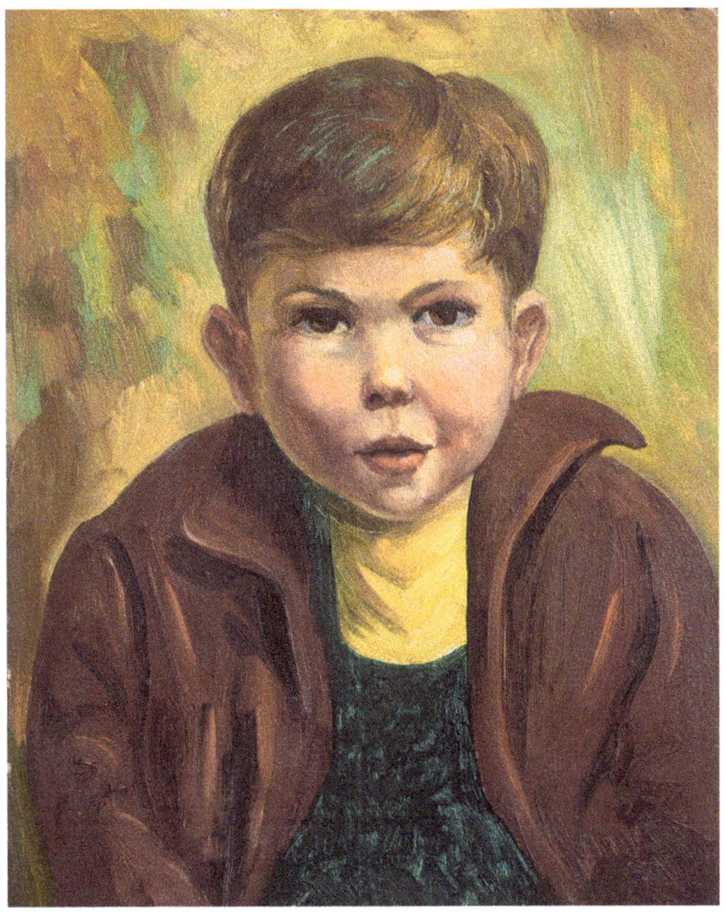

Young Charles F. Surendorf III, Nicknamed "Broozer," **16×20 (1950s).**

"Time swings swiftly when there are numerous mundane tasks to perform every day… months, even years, drown silently in a vanishing void, and the 1950s seem now an uneventful string of crushed calendars, except for the few events that punctuate the mists of apathy and boredom…," Surendorf commented years later.

In April 1956 another daughter, Cynthia Lee, was born. Charles made repeated trips to San Francisco to administer the city's outdoor art festival; these were fiscally successful events for him, and he was pleased at the opportunity to visit, talk, and exhibit with friends such as Charles Safford, Emmy Lou Packard, and Dorr Bothwell.

With a 1956 Chevrolet station wagon, the first new car Charles was ever able to buy in his career, the couple planned a road trip to Arizona and a visit to Barbara's parents. They were now near Jerome, Arizona, another abandoned mining town, which provided Surendorf endless subjects to paint. The two-week trip resulted in twenty watercolors and a block print that later won first prize in graphics at the 1957 San Francisco Art Festival.

A visit to Dick Wallach, an old friend and fellow artist in Canoga Park, California, renewed a friendship that offered a balance of eccentricity and intellectualism. In 1957 Surendorf lost another old friend when Roy Hirshburg, at age sixty-one, was murdered by a jealous woman back in Indiana.

Once again in Columbia, Barbara did all of the household work, gardening, and child-rearing chores, but Surendorf cooked the evening meal. One of his rules was refusing to have the TV on while dining. This led to furious arguments as the kids pleaded to watch TV and Barbara sided with them. The artist later produced a block print of the family, himself included, staring blankly at the TV screen.

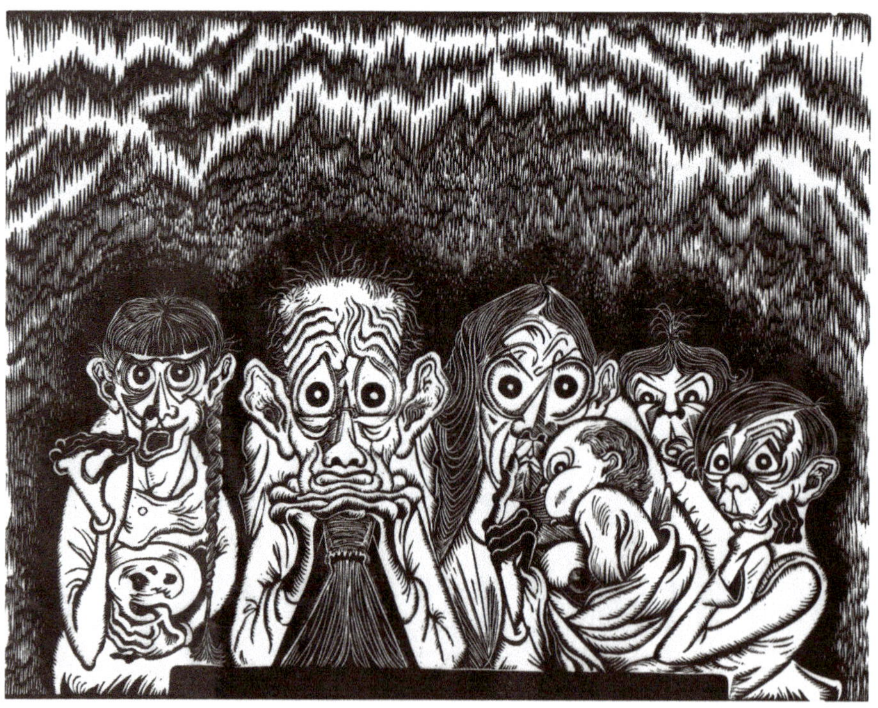

Television, **12×14.75 (1956).**

Every year, Surendorf's first wife, Natalia, dropped off daughter Karla to spend the summer with the family. Surendorf thought he was fulfilling his responsibility by sustaining a family with four kids with his output of salable art. Barbara, however, felt that she was being burdened with another child each summer. Dissension increased.

Year after year, so many people dropped in to the Columbia gallery to say hello that Charles was at a loss to know who they were. It was painfully embarrassing when an unrecognized visitor turned out to be an old student of his, a classmate from years gone by, a distant relative, an enthusiastic collector of his early works, or a woman he'd once made love to. He disliked identity-guessing games and hoped to find visitors sincerely interested in art and able to discuss it intelligently.

"Often I have been accused going out of my way to seek a confrontation that results in a controversial sideshow in the press," Surendorf recalled.

> This is not exactly true, but I do not hesitate to latch onto any action that I feel is detrimental and unjust and carry it to the city desk. I do not deliberately plot plump tidbits for public consumption, and I don't have to, because living under a bureaucratic dictatorship provides all the material for argument. It may already be construed that the state of California does not consider an artist in the confines of one of their parks, historical or recreational, to be a desirable resident or temporary tenant.

Since his San Francisco years, Surendorf retained friendships with journalists such as Herb Caen and others who loved human-interest stories of little guys taking on the state. Charles loved to fan the flames of discontent if it would generate publicity and bring people to Columbia.

By 1962 he had to move out of his old gallery space, not due to his nonconformity but because a little old lady tripped and fell on uneven floorboards, broke her hip, and sued the state for $50,000 in damages. Charles's lease said he could not make repairs without written permission from the state, which they wouldn't grant. Since he had been a thorn in the side of State Parks for eighteen years, and safety repairs were urgently needed, this was grounds for eviction. Charles was not offered any other shop space in the town's renovated structures as were other merchants. He was out and he let the world know he was being evicted. He had to support his family and pay rent on his home and he loved Columbia, so he sought unconventional solutions.

He created an "artmobile," which he parked in front of his old gallery. The Chevrolet sprouted appendages that allowed him to display paintings and prints. He had collapsible easels for art display, and signs guiding visitors to his studio on Kennebec Hill. Columbia block prints were attached to long panels of plywood and affixed to the vehicle's roof. The tailgate folded down into a display area. The state of California might control the buildings, but Tuolumne County owned the streets, and for two years Charles occupied his favorite streetcorner whenever he pleased. He got a tremendous amount of press coverage, which kept his art sales growing.

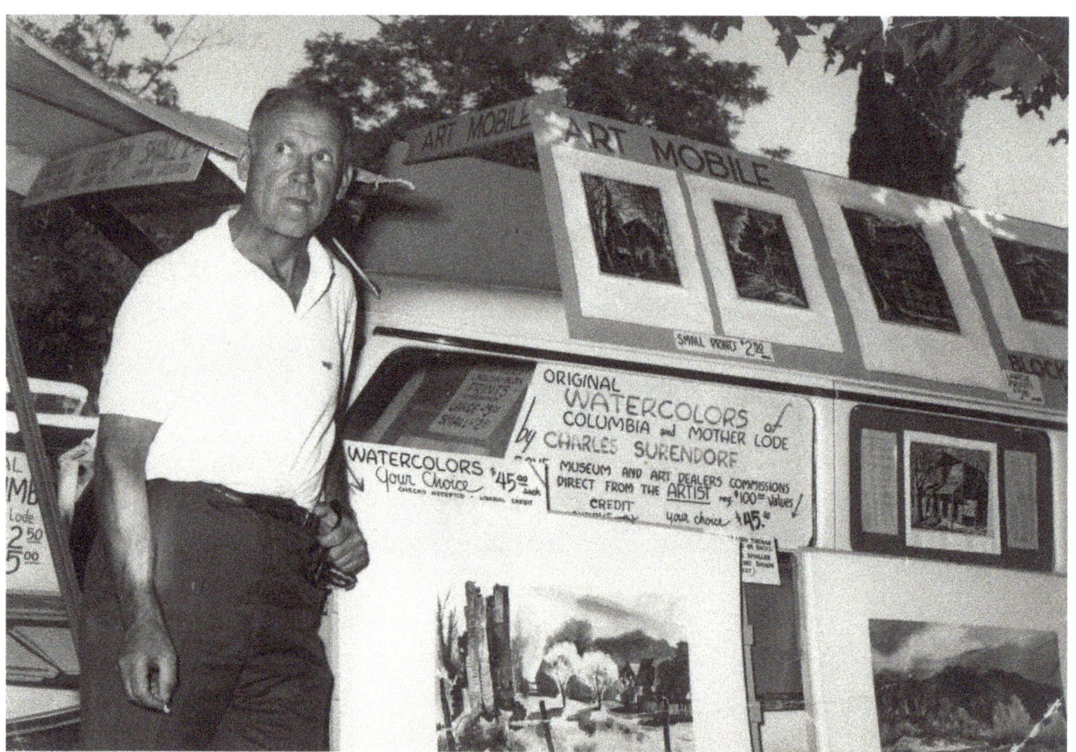

Artmobile, **Columbia, 8×10 (1960s).**

The furor around his eviction and his refusal to adopt period costume made Charles laugh. Prior to vacating the building and adapting the artmobile for sales, he had garnered nationwide and worldwide attention in the news. "I wouldn't have had any time to drink," he joked. "I was busy doing phone interviews. My gallery was so loaded with TV cameras and cables it would easily have passed for a Hollywood set." The news coverage was exaggerated, but he found it amusing.

Among the problems Surendorf had with the park administration: Carved on by generations of miners, the worn wooden benches bordering the shady sidewalks were replaced by ugly train-station benches painted brown. Surendorf adamantly refused to dress like an old gold miner, which was the standard appearance for Columbia merchants. He liked to use the term "Sierra Disneyland" for Columbia's restoration, right down to the stagecoach ride down Main Street. "To have known, loved and understood this last vestige of Americana was one of the most treasured experiences of my lifetime. To witness its final reality is the saddest. To see it embalmed and preserved in an artificial guise is the most revolting and nauseating of all acts of hypocrisy I've ever witnessed," he said.

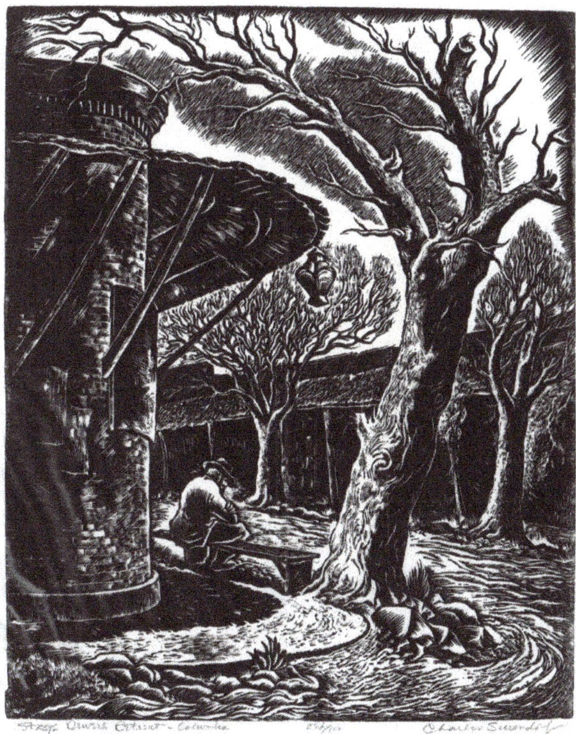

Stage Drivers Retreat, **Columbia, 11×14 (1947).**

The period of tension around the eviction had been hectic, and further defiance seemed useless. Charles had packed up his gallery in the state-owned building and left. Publicity and acclaim equate to sales and the income needed to feed a family. Surendorf had opened a gallery on his property just few blocks from downtown and outside the state park boundary. He observed, "Out of what had been a situation that foretold nothing but possible adversity, fears, and financial distress, it was resolved into a mode of living accented by peacefulness and independence."

Frustrated with bureaucracy, travel became a focus. Six weeks in Mexico with Karla—who spoke Spanish—and two more of his kids passed quickly with watercolors painted daily and new sites visited in their trusty Chevy. The trip paid for itself in a few months with sales of paintings and prints of the marketplace in Patzcuaro. Charles was happy to be out of the aesthetically doomed town of Columbia, but an unwanted family confrontation awaited him on his return.

Later, State Parks offered him a single room back in his remodeled building, mandating that he carry liability insurance, be open eight hours a day, and dress like an old gold miner. Even though the room had heat, air conditioning, and a fake chandelier in the ceiling, Surendorf noted, "The long plastered dark cavern felt like a coffin." His gallery had been the second oldest business in town after Nelson's Candy Kitchen, but now it would be history.

Surendorf Sr. died in 1962, and a financial legacy allowed plans for a family trip to Europe to move forward. The kids were given an early release from school in April, and the family took the 20th Century Limited train cross-country to New York. "The New York of 1924 and the city I knew as a student in 1927–28 was hardly the New York of 1963," Charles recalled. After visiting galleries and museums, the family boarded the USS *France* and discovered that Alfred Hitchcock was a fellow traveler. Musician and versatile songwriter Little Richard was onboard and had parties in his room. At age thirteen, Charles the III, nicknamed "Broozer," discovered marijuana—and its scent followed him everywhere.

Upon resuming drinking he claimed, "I never had a single misgiving, then or afterwards." On the ocean liner to Europe he noted:

My son was on what I believed to be a wrong track. I certainly was a damn poor example of a complete father. My devotion to the bottle was an obvious and open page in my life. I could not censor my son for smoking pot… but I had anger when he tapped my booze. Beer to bourbon was a more endangering drug than grass.

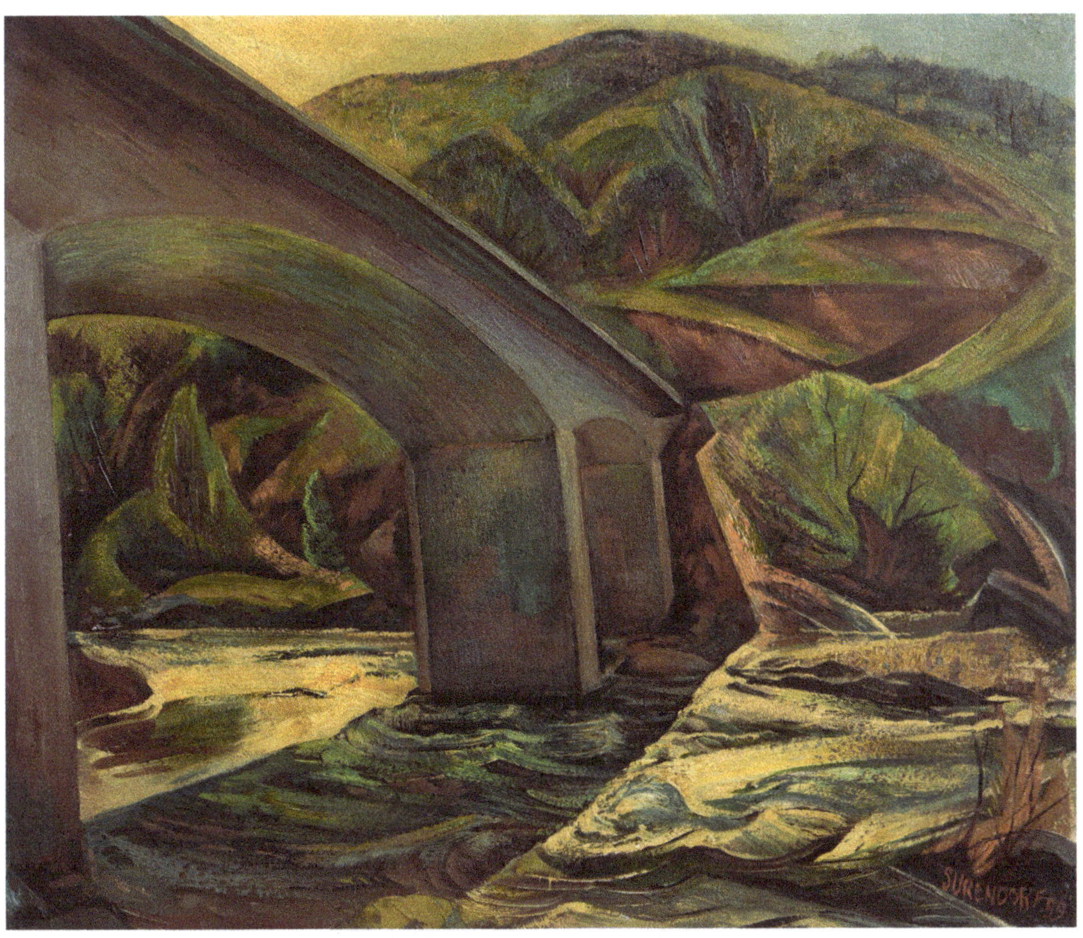

Parrotts Ferry Bridge near Columbia, **30×26 (1959). This vista is gone forever as it is now under the waters of the New Melones Reservoir.**

Unfortunately, there was a bad start to the great adventure. Every meal featured bottles of red and white wine in the center of the table. After twenty years' sobriety, Surendorf downed a full glass of wine and drank to excess for the rest of his life. In the 1970s he wrote:

It was a world I never regretted finding again. Ten years now since I drained that first glass of wine, and I have been bending my elbow with supreme relish for the entire time. There were several reasons for resisting extreme drinking, the main one being my responsibility to the children.

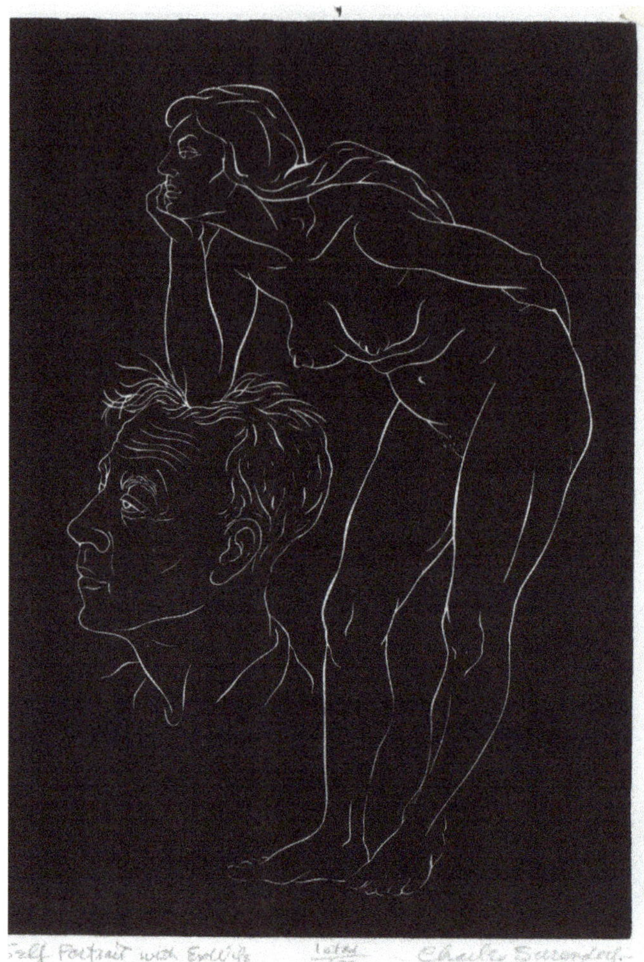

Self-Portrait with Ex-Wife, **8×12 (1967).**

The family drove 8,000 miles through Europe, and despite the fact that Surendorf had underestimated the cost of gasoline and other expenses, and had made no advanced reservations for rooms, the trip was a success.

Switzerland, Spain, and Portugal delighted them. The countryside around Arles, Van Gogh's home, was similar to the Sierra foothills, with tall swirling cypress, sun-ripened yellow grasses, and blue skies with torn clouds. Surendorf said:

The one great affection for Europe is its people, their intense respect and regard for its civilization, and the esteem held for arts and artists. Art there was not a superficial luxury reserved for the rich, it was enjoyed by everyone.

Returning to France after such lengthy travel, Barb and I felt the inevitable tourist fatigue. It was enlarged by the mistake of cooping three small children in the back seat of the MG Sports Sedan. Broozer was thirteen, Stephanie ten, and Cindy only six. Their restrained youthful exuberance exploded often among them in fights and argumentative forms that distracted me emotionally.

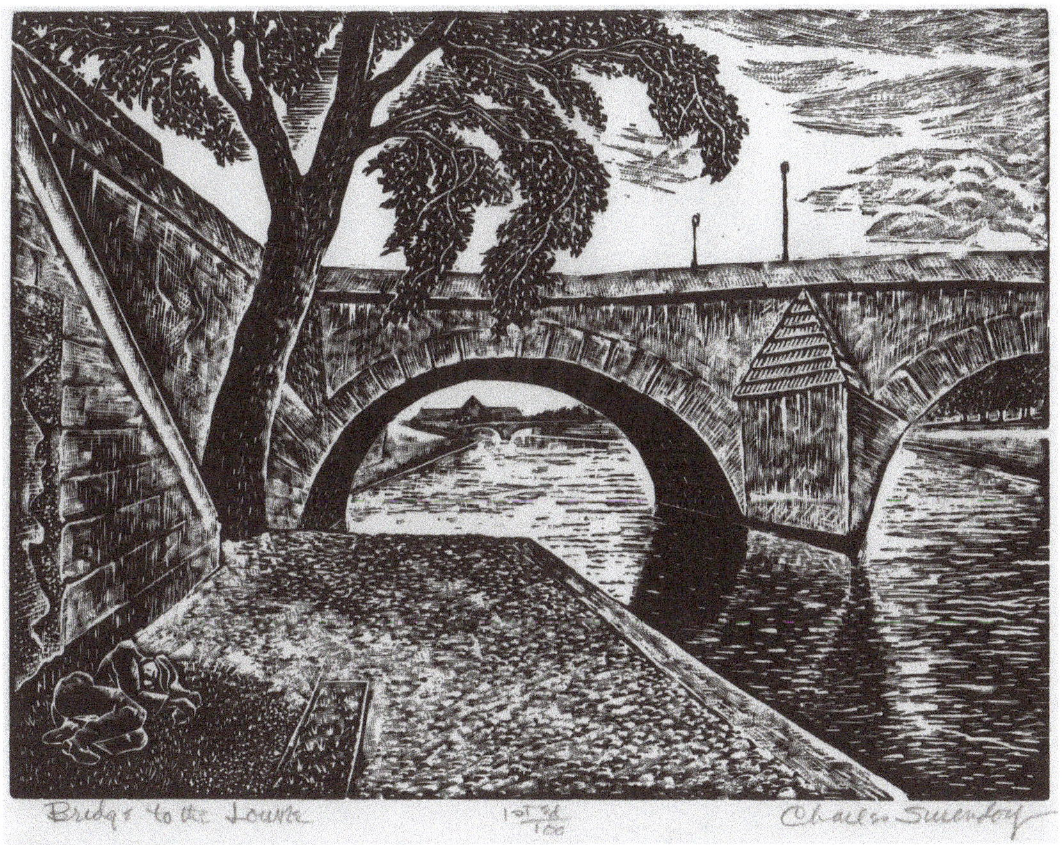

Bridge to Louvre, **France, 8×11 (1965).**

On their way home on the ocean liner, Barbara admitted to Surendorf that she'd had a sexual interlude with one of his best friends, the artist Charles Safford. She had put the foundation and the happiness of the entire family aside for a fling, Surendorf believed. He drank himself into oblivion that night. Disembarking in

New York, the Surendorf family drove back across the USA—20,000 miles of travel was over. A bright spot on the trip home was a visit with long-time friend Charles Barnes in Brown County, Indiana.

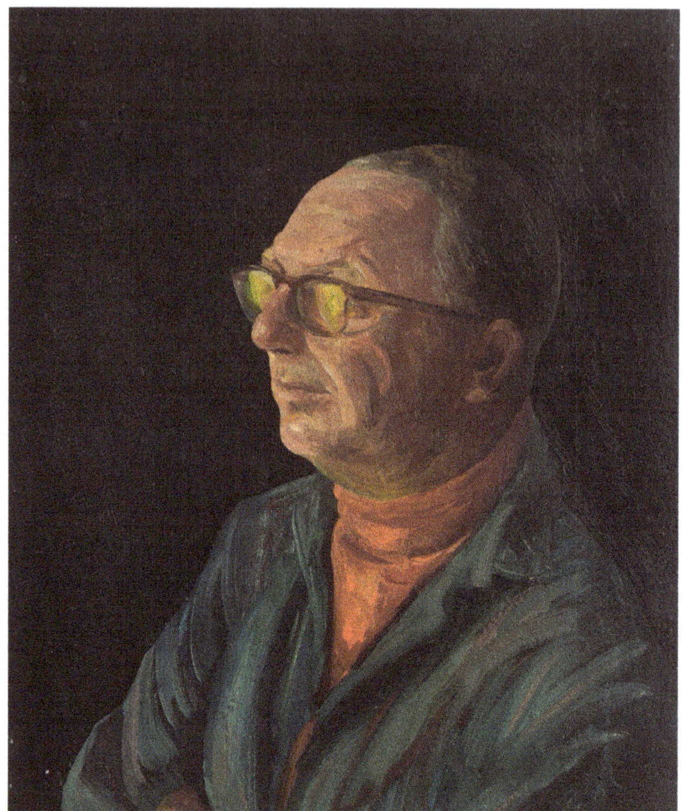

Charlie Barnes, artist and friend, **(1964).**

11: Marriage on the Rocks

Surendorf got back to painting. "Should I chance upon a tree that has been bent with storms of winter cold, its limbs twisted and reaching for the sunlight and the trunk dented and bruised by the brush of life, I am fascinated and desire to paint it," he said. Again and again these trees show up in his artwork. When he arrived in the 1930s, the town of Columbia was itself like a weathered tree. Buildings, cracked sidewalks, vacant lots strewn with building stones—all were honest. That was why he felt that the state of California and its inept amateur architects over-renovated it. He despaired that no continuing evidence of the time's passing was allowed to appear in the old town.

Settled back upon Kennebec Hill in Columbia, Charles arranged display space for his art in outbuildings and the house; various signs went up at the bottom of Maiden Lane. To Surendorf's astonishment, people began to appear every day. He had underrated the impact of all the past publicity on prospective art collectors. A narrow aisle down the middle of the barn allowed display space. "It was the damnedest gallery in the world, but it worked, and the oil paintings sold better than they did in town," he mused. If people searched out his home they were genuinely interested, and were potential customers.

Given her premarital experience at the Rotunda Gallery at the City of Paris department store in San Francisco, Barbara was the ideal assistant; she met collectors and encouraged purchases, and Surendorf paid her a commission on everything she sold, which left him free to paint, engrave, and print.

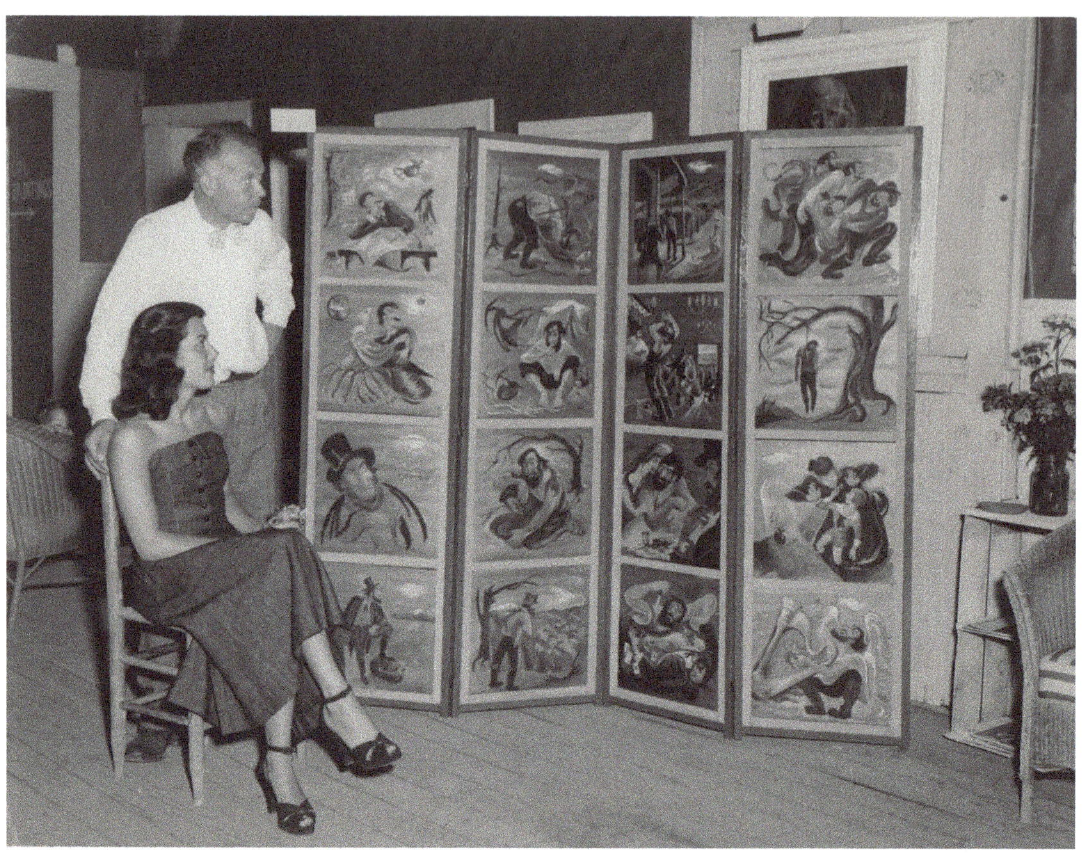

Artist and Wife and Art, **Columbia, 8×10 (early 1950s).**

While life was mostly peaceful at home, the parents meted out contradictory discipline to their kids, who grew confused. Broozer loved marijuana and was an expert at totaling cars. Surendorf Sr. considered himself a poor example of competent fatherhood; his devotion to the booze bottle clouded everything.

All through the Surendorf children's childhood in Columbia, the Fallon House Theatre became a summer center of excitement. A repertory theatre project of the University of the Pacific in Stockton, California, it allowed local young folk to be involved. Karla and Broozer played roles that called for child actors, worked as ushers, and sold soda pop during intermission. Set design, lighting, sound, and wardrobe were summer job responsibilities the Surendorf kids learned.

A couple visiting Charles's Columbia gallery extolled the virtues of New Zealand as a place to paint and sketch. A huge argument in late 1967 over some trivial family incident had him pondering a trip there with enthusiasm. It would be impossible for Barbara to come with the kids in school, and someone needed to oversee the gallery. Besides, Surendorf wanted to be alone to figure out what to do about his nonfunctioning marriage.

Artist and friend Ken Potter joined Surendorf, and daughter Karla was invited along on the trip. Queenstown Captivates American Artist, the New Zealand newspaper headline proclaimed. Lake Wakatipu has claimed another victim. The long feature story supposed Surendorf to be one of the most prominent American landscape painters, misspelled his name "Swerndorf," and regarded him as one of the top ten woodcut artists in the United States. The paper wrote that Charles's opinions were forthright but delivered without any arrogance or offense, and described him as easygoing and laconic. Surendorf was proudest that two earlier prints of his were in the book *Prized Prints of the 20th Century*. He did his work in New Zealand in watercolor because watercolors were easier to move and pack.

"You can't beat it… I've been all over the world and this tops the lot," Surendorf said of the Queenstown and Wakatipu districts. He stressed to the newspaper reporter the importance of optimism when producing art. "No one in their right mind would be an artist unless he was an optimist with a sense of humor. A true artist isn't going to paint for a customer. That's why he needs to be an optimist. I have never painted for money, I paint what I like."

After three months in New Zealand he returned to the States and found his relationship with Barabara strained. His kids were happy to see him, but his wife wasn't. Surendorf claimed she never missed a day without a drink while he spent fifteen years of their marriage sober.

Hoping to prop up an unraveling marriage, travel became another intoxicant for Surendorf. A friend had purchased several of his prints to be shipped to Mexico; Surendorf decided to deliver them himself and invite Barbara on the trip. The prints were wedding presents to be presented to the bride and groom at a ceremony planned as a notable social event. The Surendorfs were escorted around Mexico City via a limousine to the church and reception site. Charles was impressed: "The exotic pastries and seafood were so delicious I realized [that] for the first time at any party I was not devoting my attention totally to the various drinks."

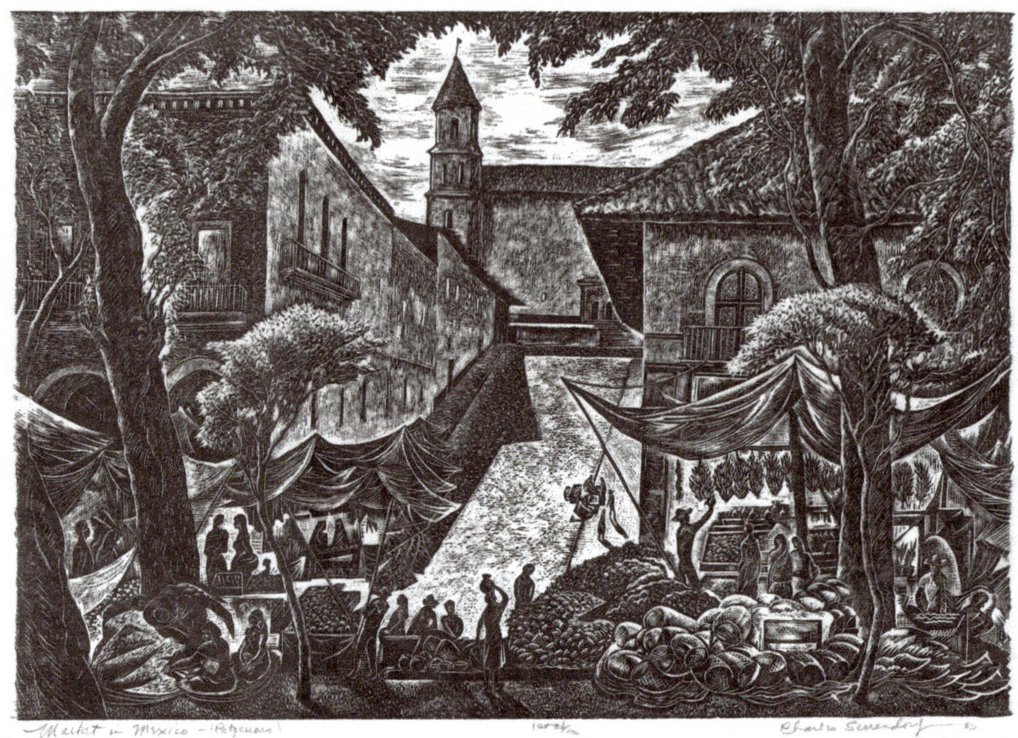

Market in Mexico, **Patzcuaro, 16.5×12 (1963).**

They enjoyed being tourists away from the children, but the pleasure was short-lived. On returning to Columbia, after yet another argument, Barbara packed up, moved out, and served Charles with divorce papers. Daughter Stephanie choose to go with Mom; Cindy, at age twelve, stayed with Dad and Broozer. Surendorf paid his divorce lawyer with a painting. The year was 1968.

The divorce triggered a series of paintings called *Romance Marriage and Divorce.* It took all summer to complete, and Charles considered it excellent therapy fueled by alcohol. "My mind was pressed with the thoughts of our divorce and painting vented them," he said. He and Barbara remained friends, and both stayed involved in their children's lives.

Another trip to Guaymas, Mexico, with a friend produced more watercolors. When stretches of solitude settled on the Mother Lode locale after tourist season, Surendorf said, "My restlessness kindled a desire to drink more than was good for me." His drinking alienated community members, and he chased customers out of his gallery if he felt they were just sightseeing rather than having any genuine attraction to his art. Of those people he said, "I felt, drunk or sober, I was worthy of consideration and interest."

Contemplating old age, Surendorf observed, "It is the companionship of artists I miss most. A relationship between artists is as necessary as the stage is to an actor. It is only through the constant meetings of sympathetic souls that one in my profession can function satisfactorily. We gave each other's ego the needed boost that painting can't."

In 1972, Surendorf took another spur-of-the-moment trip to New Zealand, eager to experience the beauty of the islands again, especially Queenstown. He was horrified to see the spread of concrete-block motels on the waterfront, and said he felt a twinge of responsibility since he'd lauded Queenstown in painting and prints for years. He rated South Island as one of the most beautiful hunks of landscape in the world, and found that the people presented a profound politeness in helping visitors.

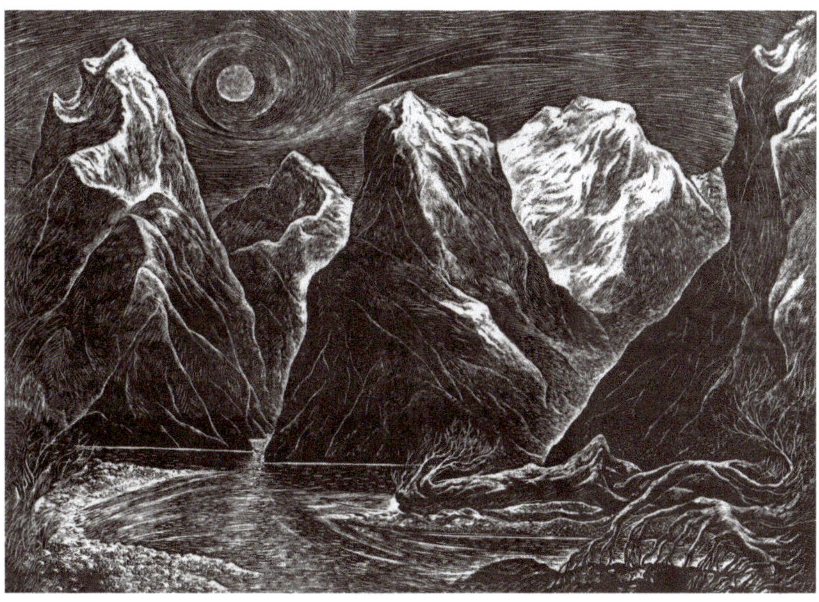

Milford Sound, **New Zealand, 16.5×10.5 (1972).**

Surendorf was a frequent visitor to the Mendocino Coast of Northern California. His son, Broozer, worked as a handyman at Little River Inn and wanted to set down roots. He purchased several acres of land in the tiny hamlet of Comptche, fifteen miles inland from the coast, and built a house around a humidity-controlled fire-proof vault that stores his father's artworks.

Father and son entertained the idea of opening a restaurant, but settled for a bakery on Kasten Street in the village of Mendocino. Due to a variety of problems it was a short-lived venture and closed in 1972.

In the fall of the that year, Surendorf found a package trip to the South Pacific that would take him to Australia, New Zealand, Bali, Singapore, Hong Kong, and Japan while daughters Cindy and Karla worked together to keep the home gallery open in Columbia.

At the stop in Tahiti, Charles stepped outside to try to capture from the air some scent of the past. It was impossible. In New Zealand he made a brief visit to Auckland, then flew on to Queenstown. The B&B he stayed in offered him a constantly changing visual banquet, and he was quick to get out his watercolors. Surendorf mused:

> I was not painting now to attempt an experiment or do a revolutionary piece of painting. What I attempted was solely for my own pleasure. No rules, preconceived plans or techniques influenced my painting, only the personal reverence I felt toward what the gods of nature had rendered.

In Australia, Surendorf admitted he often drank his dinner and then took his hangover to the pool in the morning. He went on to Bali and Singapore where he drank and picked up women for a night, then moved on. In Hong Kong he took a room at the YMCA, the institution that was so often a refuge in his life. In Kagoshima, Japan, he painted. Returning after three months' travel, he found the familiar world of Columbia comforting.

Charles never surrendered his sense of whimsy, especially when it came to Christmas trees. In 1972 he designed an upside-down tree for his gallery, and in 1974 he created an inflation tree christened *Santa Recessione*. The tree had grown two feet tall and then quit. Charles speculated it had been struck by the same malady that infected the dollar's value at the time. Any deficits in the conifer's size were more than offset by the ease and speed of decorating it. At his gallery, he had to put up a sign next to it: Please don't step on my Christmas tree.

Reflecting on his alcohol consumption at that point in his life, Surendorf said:

> Booze has a singular advantage… it's always available whereas women and

the means to travel are not. Alcoholic spirits make a springboard for certain unpredictable plunge into the calm sea of serenity. While the wind seems colder when you have to climb out, the swim is worth it.

A harbinger of old age arrived in the mail in 1974 with an announcement for the 50th-anniversary reunion of Charles's high school class in Richmond, Indiana. He mused, "Everyone is astonishingly old… they talk old, act old, and worst of all, look very old." He was, though, curious enough to attend—"My fondness for the ludicrous won out."

Surendorf refused drinks on the plane to Indianapolis, as he wanted to be able to read identification labels and memorize faces at the reunion. Seeing his classmates, he decided, "… after a half century nature's make-up man had made a total job of alterations… they could have been total strangers. The event went on with violent hand-pumping, loud laughter, and routine complimentary salutations that served to take the curse off the truth."

Always resourceful, he'd brought prints to sell to classmates, and made enough money to pay for his round-trip plane fare. He considered it an accomplishment to have escaped the event before the group singing began. His longtime friend, Roy Hirshberg, had died, and Surendorf missed him, but he was delighted that an Indiana newspaper reviewer wrote of the reunion: "In those fifty years few have changed less than Charley, who still emits the zest and zing of the early twenties."

Surendorf loved to sit at his old Royal typewriter and cogitate about the art of painting. He observed:

There is something occult and undefinable in painting nature. Often a certain area will hold you spellbound with an unknown feeling of mood and painting potentially when actually there is little or nothing in the way of material from which to form a painting. I presume the artist should then and there try to interpret the uncanny reaction he receives from what is at hand rather than make a mental note of it to transport to completion in the studio.

If one is lucky enough to be receptive to this mysterious feeling and still have all the desirable material elements to portray it, then it is inevitable that a fine painting results. Too often the artist is engulfed in the mere spectacle and pictorial ramifications of a subject when it is devoid of any personal spiritual communication. I approach nature with a reverence, respecting her diverse offerings so intensely that I wish to do her proud and in no way to belittle her enchantment with an inept interpretation. Nature is God. There is naught but nature. To be able to reflect and capture on canvas a fraction of nature's wonderful character is a gift no man should treat lightly. It is a talent rarely bestowed.

It is meant for the artist to use this blessing in a manner from which all mankind may benefit, with more of a lucid understanding of what might otherwise escape him and subtract from his life a richness, a necessity for a more acceptable life.

It is for the artist to perceive and select the most significantly beautiful and desirable aspects of life an environment, then concentrate it artfully into a permanent symbol. In a sense, a fine work of art is an idol of supreme emotional and vibrant significance. There are sacrilegious idols, to be sure, just as positive as evil, disease and death are inevitable parts of existence, yet just the makings of these idols of earthly aspects can be justified and excused as they are honest, obvious and undeniable. If a person prefers to surround himself with idols of materialistic symbols, it is then part of his freedom of choice, even though they be constant reminders of the distasteful and crass side of life.

I believe an artist's conceptions in any medium should offer mankind a fulfillment of his quest for something intangible that may be best described as a natural desire for an escape into the realm of the spiritual. The rare moments when his subconscious dwells in a dream world and sweeps away the ever present concerns of the material and mundane workaday ravage.

A work by an artist should contain the essence of the most desirable aspirations and dreams everyman seeks. It should reflect and deliver the best of nature's esthetic appeal man has ever known. It should make him happy and give the necessary inspiration to surmount the daily difficulties of living. A work of art is a fixed feeling to enjoy for the duration of its existence. It sustains confidence in the invincible purpose of man living beyond the routine of ordinary functions of humanity, of bringing a tangible ethereal conception down to earth in a concrete form where, with reverence, it may be esteemed as a man desires.

While they may sense it, most people are powerless to visualize and feel what nature holds, but do react with emotional understanding when it is concentrated to the concise statement of a work of art. It therefore stands that if the artist is by talent unqualified to transpose nature into a fixed understandable form, his efforts serve to degrade that which is originally the ultimate in a perfectional order.

The artist is at best a recorder. He is humble, but it is a humility of love. He is in command of the inner aspects of his world, and is able to appreciate with reverence its finer qualities. The man unable to fully see and record the beauty around him turns to the offerings of kindred souls endowed with talent to reveal the conception of his own evasive desires.

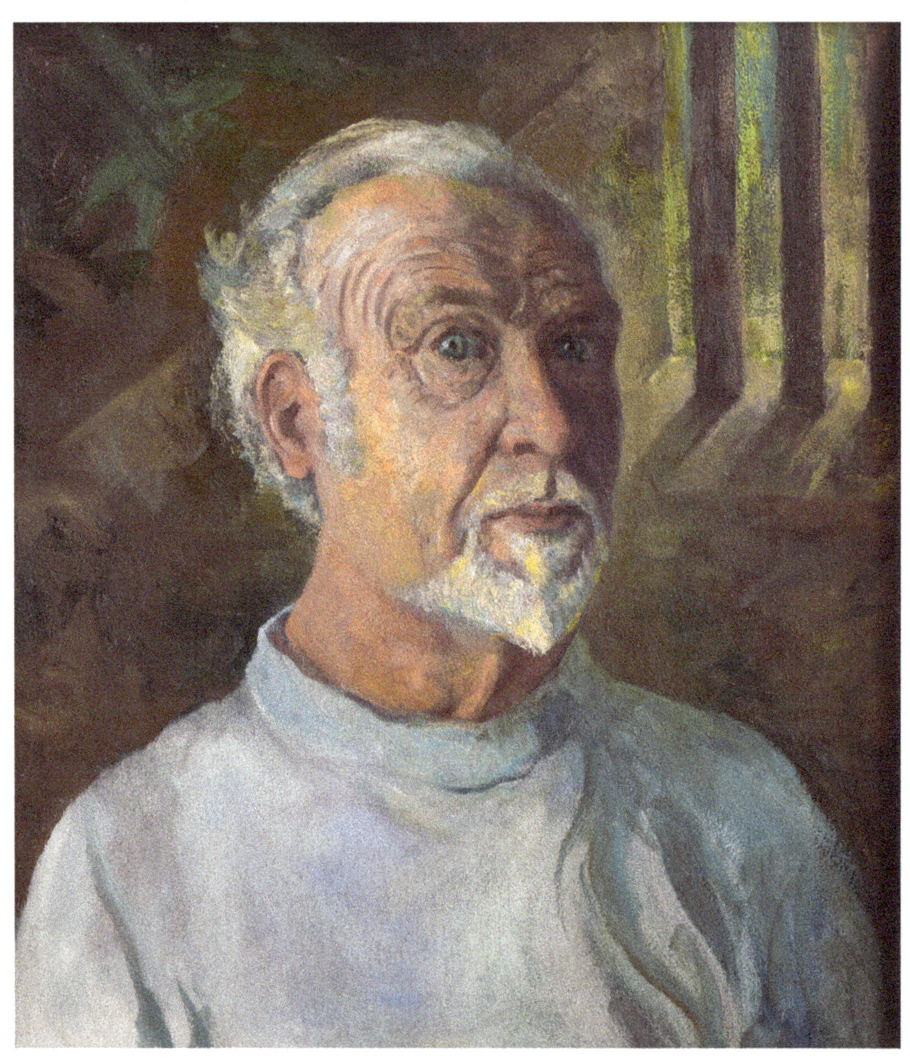

Self Portrait later in life, **24×28 (1965).**

12: Finale

Surendorf enjoyed his senior years in his ancient ramshackle home, which sat with uncertain stability on Kennebec Hill. He employed college coeds to run his homeplace gallery in a converted garage and goat shed. Cluttered, but organized, his artworks included block prints and paintings. The three scrapbooks of news clippings about himself that he had amassed over the last half-century were available for visitors to peruse.

In focusing on Columbia he echoed Vincent Van Gogh's emphasis on Arles, France. Surendorf joked:

> The only influence I got from him was unintentional, because the greens and yellows and the cypress trees here are identical to what I saw in Arles. There is a great similarity in subject matter… everything I've done has lots of movement in it… but I wouldn't cut my ear off.

Age was catching up with Charles; it inflicted arthritis and failing eyesight and the ills attendant upon fifty years of smoking Pall Malls. His children were grown and gone. He worked on his autobiography, poetry, and a novel about his misadventures with an eighteen-year-old housekeeper. When he traveled, his contributions to the *Sonora Daily Union-Democrat* were called "Travails With Charlie." For thirty years he continued to contribute witticisms to Herb Caen at the *San Francisco Chronicle*.

Surendorf still fretted at the State Park "restoration" of Columbia that robbed the town of the historic charm that the patina of age should have bestowed. He said that the state does anything that fits its commercial aspect. "They're in it to make money, and they don't give a damn about the aesthetics."

Afraid the state and the IRS could slap an inheritance tax on the value of his collection and force his family to sell it when he passed away, Charles planned to outwit them. He arranged for the best of his collection to be loaned to Columbia College for thirty years and then revert to the family—that was his solution.

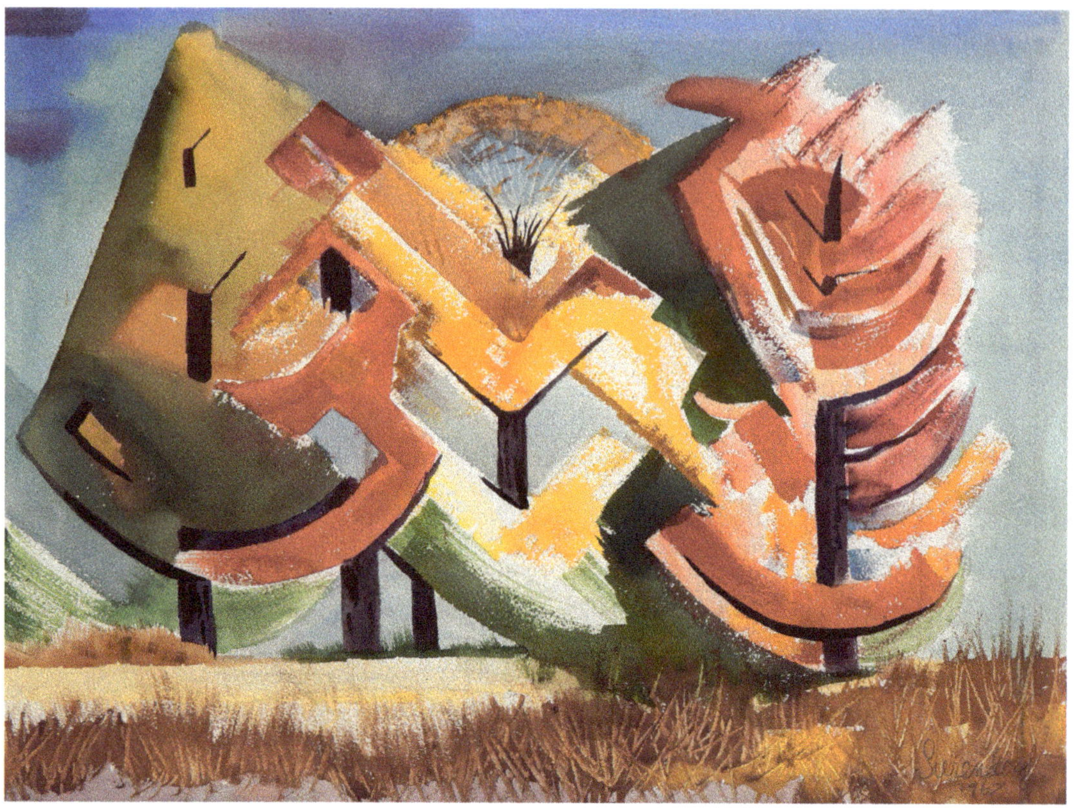

Red Autumn Trees Abstract, **18×12 (1967).**

In later years, Surendorf adopted the motto *To hell with it all.* "I believe that I have contributed a bit of richness to the world in the form of enjoyable art," he wrote. During one of his "moist" periods, when alcoholic relaxation ruled his life, he wanted to travel more. The kids were gone, he was divorced, and travel meant someone needed to run the gallery, care for the house and yard, pay the monthly bills, and keep things functioning. The answer? Advertise for a caretaker. And how did you find a female caretaker? With notes on placards posted on every bulletin board in Columbia and Sonora.

Inducements for the job listed free rent, commissions on all art sales, complete house privileges including utilities, and use of a car. Surendorf's phone rang incessantly as college coeds discovered his offer. Being young, single, and pretty were unspoken requirements. In addition to being an artist, Charles was a great storyteller, and his adventures with Michelle, the young woman he chose as caretaker, gave rise to a lively, funny read—a 200-page typed novel called *Oh Hell Michelle*. Surendorf wrote and rewrote it in his later years, but never tried to have it published.

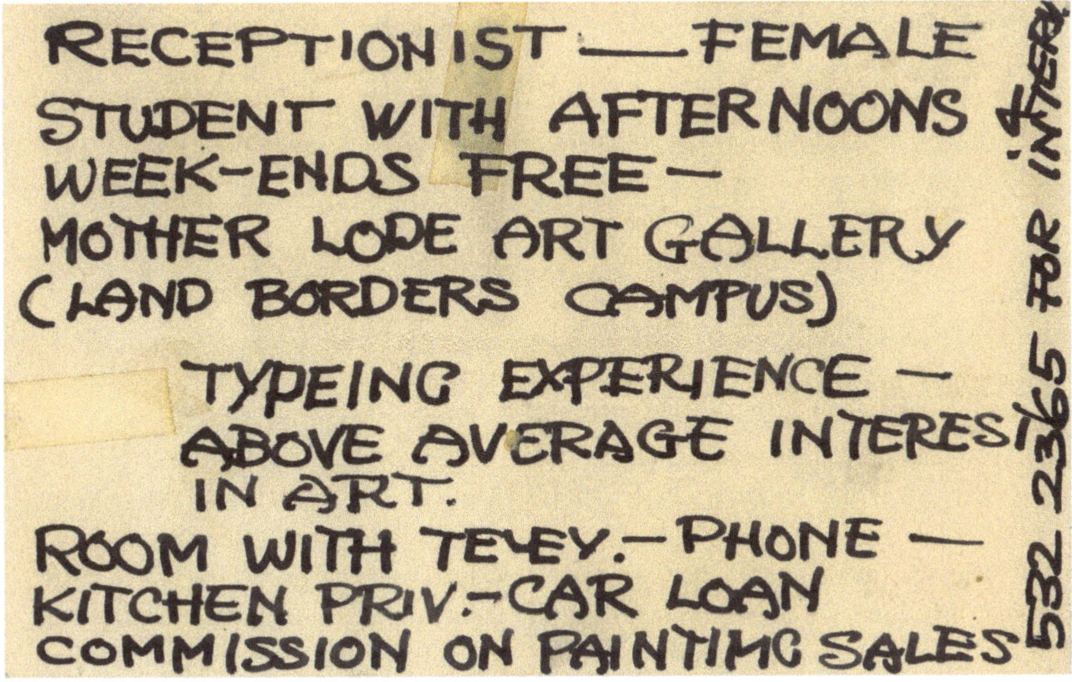

Advertisement for Studio Help, **Columbia, 5×8 (1970s).**

The Nelson family, owners of Nelson's Candy Kitchen, invited him to join them on a trip to Yugoslavia in October 1977. Arriving in Dubrovnik, Charles found a city built of stone millennia ago that was in better shape than his house back home. A room cost him $5 a night; breakfast was $1. He never developed a taste for Turkish coffee. "There is enough muck left in the bottom of the cup to plant a new crop of coffee beans," he joked.

Surendorf found the Yugoslav plum brandy excellent, and enjoyed a picnic: tourists were sailed to an offshore island for wine and barbecued fish. While painting, he attracted an audience, and to observe they stood behind him, which blocked the sunlight he needed, frustrating him.

In the years before Surendorf's death, journalists used descriptive terms such as "aging Bohemian" and "cantankerous artist" to describe him, and noted he "capitalized on misfortune." Though he dealt with the difficulties of aging, he loved living in Columbia. "The secret of the whole thing is to get yourself well known in one locality that is sufficiently large to sponsor your work so you can make a living. Then you don't have to worry as you get older; you don't have to beat your brains out," he opined.

The late 1970s saw age assail Charles. Though afflicted with arthritis, bronchitis, and failing eyesight, he never stopped typing his memoirs, poetry, a nonfiction tale, and a newspaper column. Just before a planned trip to Ireland, however, his lifelong smoking habit resulted in a diagnosis of cancer.

Charles Surendorf passed away on Kennebec Hill in Columbia on May 28, 1979. Broozer wrote this remembrance on a paper bag, still among the family's papers kept after Charles's passing. It was read graveside in the Columbia Cemetery:

We gather in this peaceful place today to thank the Lord for our father and friend Charles Surendorf, artist, Columbia. His name brought loving acknowledgement and admiration from people who knew him all over the world. Our place with Charlie is special in that we have gotten to know him and love him. Though we put Charles to rest more than his memory will live on. He wanted to die exactly as he did—with his loved ones at his side. We are grateful he passed on quietly and without pain with the knowledge he was being cared for and loved by his by those closest to him. We are blessed to know the joy of Dad's passing. He raised us all to carry on as Surendorfs, a name for which we will forever be proud. As we lay Charles to rest, we rejoice that his spirit will always be in our hearts. Thank you, Lord, for our father and friend Charles Surendorf.

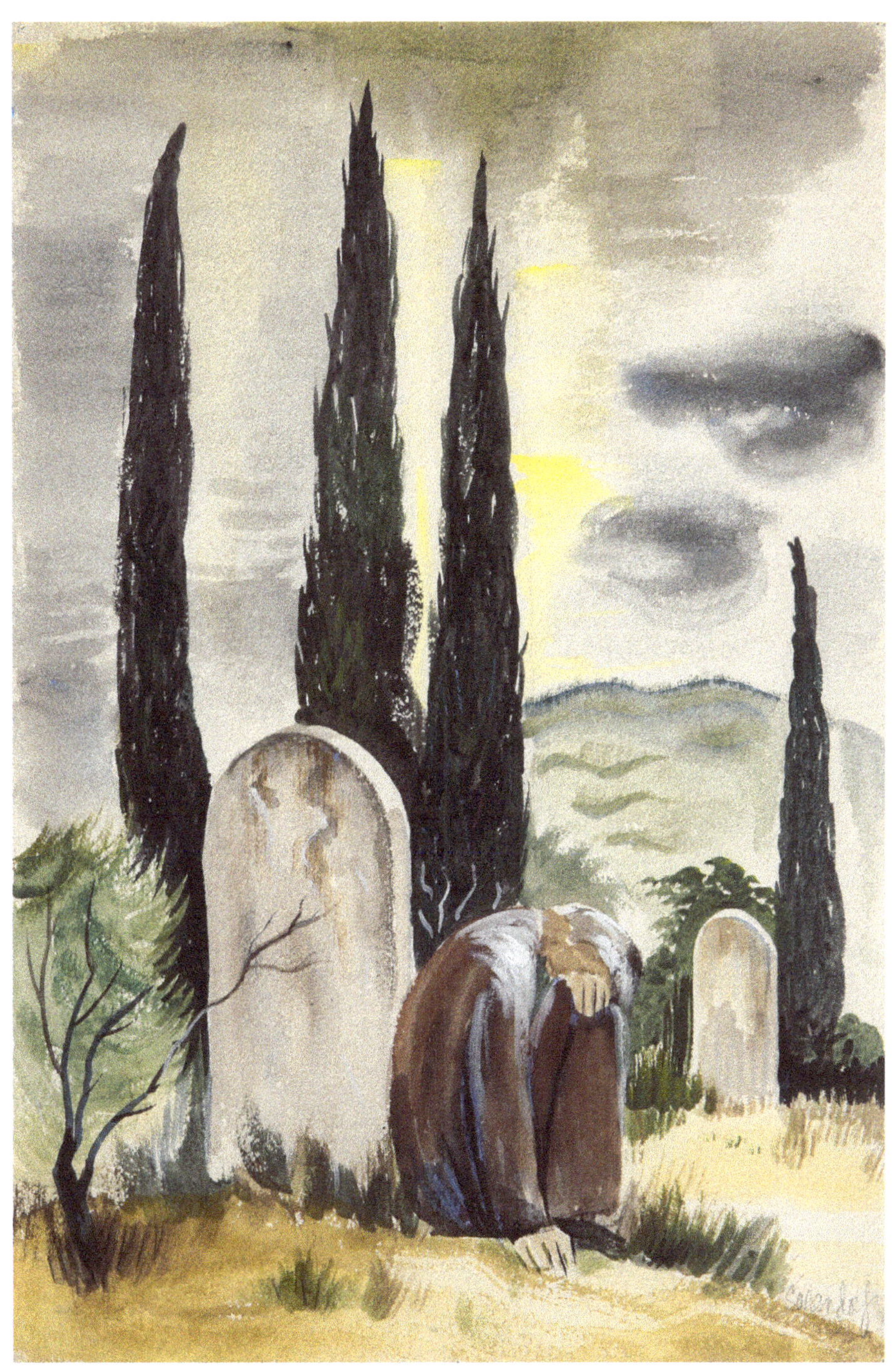

Graveyard, **13×20 (nd).**

Surendorf's Poetry

From an unpublished collection of Surendorf's poetry titled *Poems Con Tequila or Booze and Broads* come these contributions:

How Hard
the new moon tries
to escape the black velvet
boundary
of nights hypocrisies
opaque clouds living
shapeless as doom
soon to die
remembered
brightly for a spell
as it cried a mellow light

Now the earth aglow
caverns of doom below
Dispelled by night
of Another Light
The Invincible power
of Love
When I think
about you
I sorta
want to
Reach out
In the air
and pull
you in
from now here

I was loving
her
and she was
loving me
Between the
two of us
we got three

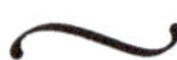

Why are palm trees crooked
leaning this way and that
Because they love each other
And can't see where they're at

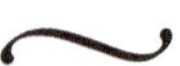

I painted her
With great delight
Sensing each brush stroke
Had magic sight

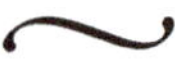

You turn love
on and off
like Burners
on off
on off
like burners
on the range
that ranges
far and wide
and
on and off

Often I burn
my fingers
holding the match
while your light
lingers

Your smile
I carry
For awhile
Like a
Parcel of butterflies
Destined for
Some Distant Isle

Artistic Achievements

Charles F. Surendorf was a member of the California Society of Etchers, the San Francisco Art Association, and the Bay Region Art Association (Oakland).

Charles F. Surendorf exhibited at the Los Angeles County Museum of Art (1936), San Francisco Museum of Art (1936–1946), California Society of Etchers (1938–1954), Golden Gate International Exposition (1939), deYoung Museum (1946), and the Art Institute of Chicago, National Academy of Design.

Charles F. Surendorf's works were in the permanent collections of the Library of Congress, San Francisco Museum of Modern Art, Mills College (Oakland), Monterey Peninsula Museum, Wichita Art Museum, Frederick Remington Art Museum, University of Minnesota, Print Club of Albany, New York, St. Louis Art Museum, Achenbach Foundation of San Francisco, Smithsonian Institute, and the California State Library.

Acknowledgments

Any book reflects the work of a team. I would like to thank Ree Slocum and Morning Glory Graphics for reproducing the art; Maria Goodwin for editorial assistance; Jane Oros for typing three books for me now; and Cypress House for putting the book together.

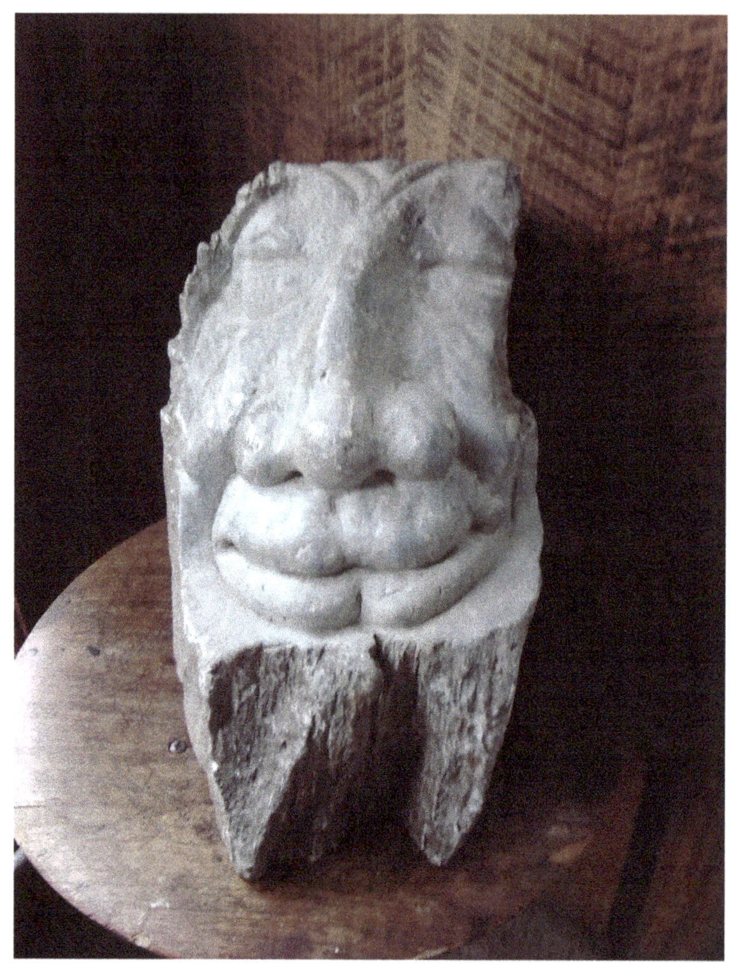

Late in life, Surendorf created a bust of Bacchus carved in soapstone.

"Let us consider ourselves beside Bacchus, God of wine…. Realize the inspiration of fine wine, a deep, though everlasting indulgence," says Surendorf's son Charles F. Surendorf III. "When leaving the Surendorf Gallery, a sign at the bottom of the driveway said, ALL PASSES, ART ALONE ENDURES."